| DATE DUE | | | |
|---|---|---|---|
| FEB 21 | | | |
| | | | |
| | | | |
| | | | |
| | | | |
| | | | |
| | | | |
| | | | |
| | | | |
| | | | |
| | | | |
| | | | |

# LAND USE
# AND ABUSE

# LAND USE AND ABUSE

BY D. J. HERDA AND
MARGARET L. MADDEN

SERIES CONSULTANT:
CHARLES R. BARMAN

FRANKLIN WATTS
A Science/Technology/Society Book
New York London Toronto Sydney 1990

Photographs courtesy of: United Nations: pp. 18, 75, 94 (AID/Purcell),
123 (Nagata); Photo Researchers: pp. 21 (Allan D. Cruickshank),
23 (Union Pacific R.R.), 64 (George Porter), 69 (USDA), 72 (Joe Munroe),
78 (Horst Bielfeld), 87 (Karl Wiedmann), 103 (Tom McHugh),
106 (Stephen J. Krasemann), 113 (Spencer Grant), 118 (Ray Ellis),
124 (Barbara Rios); National Park Service: p. 28 (Richard Frear);
Wide World Photos: pp. 31, 57, 59, 77, 121; Forest Service Collection,
National Agricultural Library: p. 84.

Library of Congress Cataloging-in-Publication Data

Herda, D. J., 1948–

Land use and abuse / by D. J. Herda and Margaret L. Madden.
p.   cm.—(A Science/technology/society book)
Includes bibliographical references and index.
Summary: Describes the environmental impact of land use, showing how careless
development leads to loss of agricultural lands and animal and plant species and
causes deforestation, desertification, and urban sprawl.
ISBN 0-531-10953-4
1. Land use—Environmental aspects—Juvenile literature.   2. Agricultural
ecology—Juvenile literature.   3. Land use—Environmental aspects—United
States—Juvenile literature.   4. Agricultural ecology—United States—Juvenile
literature.
[1. Land use.]   I. Madden, Margaret L.   II. Title.   III. Series.
HD111.H47   1990
363.73'96—dc20                                        90-37573   CIP   AC

# CONTENTS

# LAND USE
# AND ABUSE

# CHAPTER 1
# SCIENCE AND TECHNOLOGY

A mural in the dome of the National Academy of Sciences' Great Hall in Washington, D.C., depicts the history of science. Beneath the mural reads this inscription:

> *To Science, pilot of industry, conqueror of disease, multiplier of the harvest, explorer of the universe, revealer of nature's laws, eternal guide to truth.*

It's quite a tribute, but, in the case of science, it's justified.

From the earliest days of civilization to our present era of nuclear energy and space-age technology, science, the knowledge of facts and laws, has been coveted more highly than gold. And rightfully so. Gold can buy only a limited number of things and appreciate in value at only a marginal rate; scientific knowledge can buy access to the seas, sun, and stars—to our very universe—and appreciate thousands of times within the blink of an eye.

Like the links in a chain, the discovery of one scientific fact invariably leads to another. On the heels of scientific discovery comes technology: applying science to a practical end. Each time a new scientific fact is discovered, new technological developments often follow.

When the German physicist Heinrich Hertz discovered the existence of electromagnetic waves, a scientific fact, the American inventor Thomas Edison went to work designing a means of putting that discovery to work in inventing the electric light bulb, a technological achievement. Building on that success, Edison went on to design the world's first electrical lighting and power system—another technological achievement—followed by the first central electric-light power plant, still another. Hertz's initial discovery of electrical impulses led to an entirely new world of technological achievements.

Edison's remarkable technological achievements were prompted by curiosity, of course, as well as a burning desire to succeed. Like every other human being on earth, he was spurred to secure his physical, mental, and emotional well-being. Without that need, science and technology might have gone the way of the dinosaur or the dodo long ago.

Whereas mankind required a hundred thousand years to evolve to the point of the industrial revolution, each major revolution since has come in an increasingly shorter period of time. Some of the reasons are an increase in governmental and industrial support for scientific research; the availability of more sensitive scientific measuring instruments; and the increased access to more powerful computers and electronic information-storing systems for the faster acquisition and analysis of data.

Whereas evolution required millions of years to reach a point whereby *Homo sapiens* acquired the knowledge and ability to sail a ship halfway around the world, it took fewer than five centuries more to develop the ability to place a man on the surface of the moon.

Similarly, mankind required 100,000 years of evolution to stumble to the doorway of the information revolution with the invention of Sperry Univac's first mainframe computer, a machine so large and complex that it literally filled a large room to overflowing and broke down every few minutes. Yet, it has taken fewer than fifty years more to bring the information revolution to more than a third of the men, women, and children on the face of the earth.

## TECHNOLOGICAL PARITY

Today hundreds of millions of people around the world have the ability to send and receive telephone calls and electronic mail, shop for daily meals, rent a car, deposit weekly paychecks, buy and sell stocks and bonds, and make airline reservations—all in a matter of minutes—from the comfort of their own homes.

This is one of the peculiarities of technology: technological parity, or the tendency of a major advance in science or technology to spread quickly around the world.

In the early Renaissance years of the fifteenth century, the discovery of gunpowder and cannons allowed a few technologically enlightened kings and princes to control entire continents of people.

Only the wealthiest, most powerful rulers had the ability to arm and train enough men in the use of cannons and muskets to form armies capable of battering down their enemies' walls and shooting their armored knights with muskets.

But technological developments in the field of armaments increased rapidly. Before long, farmers as well as kings shared the same deadly firepower. By the year 1815, Andrew Jackson's ragtag assembly of Americans was able to defeat a strong, professional British army at New Orleans in the War of 1812. The Americans had acquired the technology to produce accurate, long-range rifles, whereas the British had contented themselves with the use of old-fashioned scatter-shot muskets. That's technological parity.

During the waning months of World War II, American scientists worked hard at developing the armament to end all armaments, the atomic bomb. When President Truman ordered the bomb dropped on the Japanese cities of Hiroshima and Nagasaki, the war quickly came to a halt. Truman later declared that such deadly technology must never escape into the hands of other nations. Yet, today, more than a dozen countries are capable of building and using such a bomb against their neighbors. Should this ability fall into the hands of an unscrupulous leader or a terrorist organization set upon destroying society, the results could be disastrous. That's another example of technological parity.

## A DOUBLE-EDGED SWORD

Some people blame our problems on science and technology. They'd like to halt technological advancement in its tracks and somehow end our reliance on science, turning back the clock to a simpler time when such problems didn't exist.

But imagine what the world would be like today if we suddenly shut down all the research laboratories in the world; all the science and engineering colleges; all the factories, engineering offices, and electrical power plants; all the automobiles, trucks, trains, planes, and ships using engines of any sort. Imagine a world without electricity, without radio and television, without tractors and chemical fertilizers, computers, telephones, plastics, antibiotics, air-conditioning, and central heating.

If all these products of modern science and technology were eliminated today, nearly everyone in the world would be dead within a very short period of time. Billions of human beings would starve to death as the world's farm produce failed to reach its markets. Those people who were fortunate enough not to starve would likely die from unchecked diseases. A world without science and technology would be no Garden of Eden, but rather a Death Valley.

The global community today finds itself in a serious dilemma. We can't live without science and technology. Yet, if they are misused, we can't live with them, either. So are science and technology good or evil? The answer is simple: they're both. *People* determine how science and technology are used: for good or evil. A rifle shell, after all, has no sense of morality, but the person aiming it can kill.

Human beings, like other living organisms, have always polluted their environment with the by-products of their actions. As living organisms, they create wastes from their digestive and metabolic systems. As social beings, they remove things from the environment; change them to suit their housing, clothing, food, and recreational needs; and return their by-products, including harmful pollutants, to the environment.

As long as population density remains low, the environment is able to accommodate these by-products. When the population density becomes too high, deterioration of the natural environment—our air, water, and soil—takes place, often at an alarming rate.

Although high population density is a major problem in causing pollution, it's not the only problem. As populations grow in size, they also demand higher standards of living. These ever-increasing demands place even greater strains on the earth's natural resources.

Over the years, mankind has overpowered the environment with both his numbers and his misplaced technology. One of the greatest examples of this tragedy is mankind's use—and *abuse*—of the land on which humanity relies for its very life.

How long can man continue to do so before the land is irreparably damaged? Many scientists believe the time is frighteningly close at hand.

# CHAPTER 2
# THE HISTORY OF LAND USE

If you were to turn on your television set to watch a special thirty-minute program about the history of life on earth, you'd view minute after minute of amazingly beautiful mosses and lichens and ferns and grasses followed by the emergence of strange and remarkable animals from the seas, animals that eventually grew legs and feet and began breathing air into remarkably complex new organs called *lungs*.

You'd witness the evolution of reptiles and the development of dinosaurs, followed by both small and large mammals. You'd see animals flying through the air and crawling on the ground, climbing over rocks, and swinging through the trees. Finally, in the last *3.5 seconds* of the program, you'd witness the birth and entire existence of mankind.

It's remarkable to think that *Homo sapiens*, human beings, have populated the planet for so short a period of earth's life—approximately 100,000 of its billions of years of existence—but it's true. Yet, human beings have made more of an impact on the planet than any other creature since the beginning of time.

## HUMAN ADAPTATIONS

The German philosopher Nietzsche once observed, "Every animal except man has a well-defined habitat." Birds inhabit the trees; bats live in caves; deer roam the forests. Yet, man can live virtually anywhere he chooses, from one pole to the other, from one end of the globe to the next. He can make his home in houses and huts, in tents and tepees, from the hot, humid climate of the tropics to the frigid cold of the Arctic. The reason for this remarkable flexibility is technology. Over the years, man has learned to use his superior intellect to adapt the world around him to meet his living requirements and thus extend his range to wherever he desires. But it wasn't always so.

Various anthropological findings, studies based on layers of debris from past cultures buried in the earth, show that early *Homo sapiens* relied on hunting and gathering of available food to survive. In so doing, he often had to cover enormous areas of territory. As man discovered fire and techniques to control it, he gained an advantage over the rest of the animals on earth. One of his earliest hunting techniques involved the use of fire as a tool.

After locating an area rich in wildlife, a group of hunters would set fire to the area. Several hunters would lie in ambush for the animals, which would be slaughtered as they emerged from the woods. Later, after the fire had died down, the hunters would walk through the ashes, collecting the burned carcasses of those animals caught in the flames.

By manipulating nature in this way, man first learned that he was capable of making life on earth less toilsome and more productive. Later still, he discovered that, by capturing and taming certain animals, he could not only provide himself with meat, hides, and wool but also with milk, butter, and cheese. In so doing, he discovered that it was much less work to follow domesticated cattle, sheep, and goats around a field than to chase elusive wild game through the forests.

But that led to problems. Although mankind no longer had the need to range far and wide in search of food, his flocks of domesticated animals eventually grazed beyond the grassland's ability to recover and both herd and herdsman were forced to move to greener grazing lands.

This proved a particularly critical problem in the Middle East and along the Mediterranean coast, where the land originally supported sprawling forests and a good growth of grass on the mountain slopes and plains. The Greek author Homer, writing around 900 B.C., described lush, thick stands of tall pines and oaks growing around the island of Sicily (now part of the country of Italy).

But constant grazing by growing flocks of sheep and goats eventually destroyed the young seedlings needed to replace the old trees as they died. Soon, *all* the trees were gone. As grazing pressure on the land increased, even the grass disappeared. Without trees and grass to hold the soil on the mountainous slopes in place, severe soil erosion soon set in.

Today, much of the rich soil that once covered

Both overgrazing and erosion are land-use
problems in Mediterranean countries. The
famous "cedars of Lebanon" reappeared on the
mountainsides of Lebanon as a result of that
country's reforestation program during the 1960s.

the Mediterranean countryside lies in deep layers in heavily silted rivers and deltas. The steep mountain slopes are stripped down to bedrock in many parts of Turkey, Greece, Yugoslavia, Italy, Spain, and North Africa. The economic value of the grasslands and forests has been lost to erosion forever.

In other parts of the world, early farmers were learning that they could plant the seeds of certain crops in order to produce new generations. Observing that the healthiest plants in nature often grew from the ashes of fires started by lightning, farmers soon began setting fire to the prairies and planting their seeds in the ash-enriched soils that resulted. In this way, they learned to increase both the quantity and the quality of their harvests.

Fire, too, took man beyond simple agricultural and domestic uses by opening for him the age of metals. The chance discovery of simple metals melting in a hot campfire, then cooling to tremendous hardness, opened the door to new and improved agricultural implements, as well as to increased agricultural production.

By the time the early European pioneers began settling the colonies of North America's Plymouth and Jamestown, thoughts of agricultural conservation were still limited to extremely basic questions. Would the wild turkeys and deer last the winter? Would the settlers have to haul firewood from some distant area? As time passed and the population of the New World boomed, resources close at hand had been exhausted and the settlers were forced to travel farther and farther from home to locate replacements.

When land, timber, game, and other natural resources up and down the Atlantic seaboard became scarce, many settlers simply abandoned their homes and farms and moved west across the Appalachian Mountains; then out into the lush, green Ohio River valley; and finally across the prairies and Rockies of central North America to the Pacific coast. As they traveled, they left behind a large swath of felled trees, depleted soils, and eroding pasturelands. Huge herds of American bison, deer, and other game animals had all but vanished. The Indians who had lived in peace and harmony with nature for thousands of years were forced off their own lands and pushed to the very brink of extinction.

When the settlers finally used up all the readily available resources and exhausted the last of America's open frontiers, they began thinking more seriously about the concept of conservation. But was it soon enough?

## THE NEW NATION

After the Revolutionary War of 1776 established the new republic, a new land ordinance made it possible for the young government to sell its publicly held lands to various individuals. Another act in 1796 provided that land should be auctioned to the highest bidders in sections (640 acres to the section) at a minimum price of two dollars an acre. Sales were slow, though, because the government had placed on the market more land than available consumers could purchase. As a result, squatting— private citizens' building homesteads on unoccupied public land—became commonplace.

As more and more people took to squatting, pub-

The American bison, once brought to the verge of extinction by the reckless march of westward expansion, has made a comeback in recent years.

lic policy grew to accept them. The Preemption Act of 1841 gave squatters the right to purchase at a minimum price the land on which they had squatted before it was put up for sale at public auction. Squatting continued to play a major force in the settlement of American lands for several decades. But the effects of squatting continued well into the next century.

Since squatting was an easy way to acquire free land, squatters often held the land and its resources in low esteem. Once a family of squatters had cleared the forests and stripped the fields of their minerals and other nutrients, removed the fish from the streams, and chased the game from the woods, they simply pulled up stakes and moved on to more promising lands.

President Abraham Lincoln attempted to reinstill Americans' pride of land ownership with the signing of the Homestead Act of 1862. This act provided a 160-acre parcel of land to anyone who would live on and care for it for five years. About 1.5 million homesteading claims were filed under this act during the nineteenth century, giving new hope to poor families who could not otherwise afford to own their own land.

Besides granting free land to anyone willing to live on and work it, the federal government was extremely generous in providing free land to the nation's newly born railroads, ultimately deeding more than 180 million acres to various railroad companies, as well as to states for use in constructing railroad rights-of-way. It was an effort to open up the West as quickly as possible with little or no thought to the environmental consequences.

During the 19th century, the U.S.
government deeded millions of acres to
various railroad companies. This directly
subsidized the opening of the West.

## DESTRUCTION OF FORESTS

Meanwhile, forests were falling throughout the United States for still other reasons. Prior to the discovery of coal as a fuel, the major source of energy was wood. Settlers often cut down entire forests to provide fuel to heat their homes. During the industrial revolution, such industries as ironworking, glassmaking, and pottery production began using large quantities of charcoal, a relatively clean-burning by-product of wood, to provide energy to produce their products.

As the forests closest to towns and cities disappeared, farmers moved their cattle, sheep, and goats out into the newly cut lands to graze. In a short time, the animals ate the remaining vegetation down to the last twig, ensuring no new tree growth there for many years to come.

As continuing demands for charcoal reduced forests to barren wastelands, wood to fire the furnaces of industry had to be hauled in from greater distances, opening up even more forestlands to grazing and agricultural loss. Finally, the demand for charcoal could no longer keep pace with its use by industry. A new fuel was needed, and it was found. Soon, men and machines were digging large holes in the ground from which they were extracting coal and ore.

In order to extract coal, which often lay far below layers of rich topsoil, soft rock, and shale, miners began digging deep holes, piling the soil, rock, and shale in gigantic mounds beside the pit. When the last of the coal had been removed, the miners abandoned the pit and moved on to another site. Entire mountainsides, valleys, and streams were disrupted so badly that any economic or recreational use was impossible. The soil surrounding the excavation site was often so acidic from minerals leaching from the exposed diggings that very few plants could grow there. The area became a giant wasteland.

## EARLY ENVIRONMENTALISTS

Then, around the end of the Civil War, George Marsh, the father of modern conservation, wrote and published a book entitled *Man and Nature: Of Physical Geography as Modified by Human Action.* The book became a conservation classic, warning mankind that America's natural resources could no longer be exploited without concern for the future. As long as humanity continued on its foolish path to self-destruction, Marsh argued, it would never realize the benefits from the asethetic, scientific, and spiritual values of nature.

Marsh explained the balance of nature and the interrelationships between man and his environment by describing the ecological effects of draining lakes and swamps; the effects of canals, dams, and wells on aquatic life, water tables, and plant succession; the influence of forests on soil and weather; and the effects of drifting sands on the Suez Canal project, which was well under way. In short, Marsh burst a bubble: the assumption that nature's resources were inexhaustible. A new attitude toward American conservation was beginning to develop.

But despite the pleadings of Marsh, John Wesley Powell, and other environmentalists of the day, Congress failed to take any major steps toward protecting America's lands until it passed a rider attached to a public lands bill in 1891. The rider gave the president the power to set aside certain forested lands as public reservation areas. Within months after the 1891 congressional session, 33 million acres of land was withdrawn from sale and became part of the first of our forest preserve systems, later to be renamed national forests. Shortly after that, America's first national parks, Yellowstone and Yosemite, were founded.

Soon thereafter, several conservationists began conducting private surveys regarding the condition of our public lands. Such men as Henry David Thoreau, Aldo Leopold, Robert Marshall, and John Muir wrote extensively, and their books and papers found a receptive audience not only in America but throughout the world. In 1892, Muir founded the Sierra Club, which was dedicated to "exploring, enjoying and rendering accessible the mountain regions of the Pacific Coast." In 1932, Marshall organized the Wilderness Society, which became an articulate and leading voice for supporters of wilderness recognition, later playing a major role in pressuring Congress to pass the Wilderness Act of 1964.

In 1905, President Theodore Roosevelt, a dedicated conservationist, declared that the object of forestry was not to "lock up" forests but to "consider how best to combine use with preservation." Three years later, on May 13, 1908, he invited a thousand national and state leaders to the White House for a three-day conference on conservation. The conference was organized by Gifford Pinchot, who promoted the idea that the nation's forests could be held in the public domain and used at the same time.

Forests were valuable renewable resources, he argued, when properly managed and harvested.

In opening the conference, Roosevelt said, "Let us remember that the conservation of our natural resources, though the gravest problem of today, is yet but a part of another and greater problem to which this Nation is not yet awake . . . the problem of national efficiency."

Although no legislation resulted from the conference, it did succeed in crystallizing public opinion about the need for conservation of our national lands. After the conference, twenty-three states created departments of conservation. For the first time in history, the general public displayed serious concern about damages done by environmental raiders and the special interests of corporate America.

During the Taft administration following Roosevelt's term in office, two far-reaching conservation measures joined those already on the books. The Weeks Act of 1911 authorized a system of national forests in the eastern part of the country, and the National Park Service Act of 1916 cleared the way for the establishment of a series of national parks overseen by paid professional park administrators and conservation specialists.

The 1920s saw the development of many resource management programs. Among the most effective was the concept of county planning, pioneered in California. As urbanization, the spread of major urban centers farther out into rural lands, continued at a frightening pace, various counties appointed board members to review and restrict land use in an effort to control growth and protect natural resources.

View in Yosemite National Park.
The National Park Service Act
of 1916 grew out of the efforts
of early conservationists.

## THE NEW DEAL ERA

It wasn't until the Great Depression of the 1930s that various governmental programs designed to make the most efficient use of our natural resources were born. Within months of assuming office, President Franklin D. Roosevelt helped pass two of the best known conservation acts in American history, creating the Tennessee Valley Authority (TVA) and the Civilian Conservation Corps (CCC).

The TVA was the most sweeping resource management program in American history. It soon became the byword for the concept of regional planning throughout the world. Originally established to oversee the management of natural resources within the Tennessee River drainage basin, it eventually grew to be a model for a new regional concept of total resource management: retaining local resources for the local population.

The CCC was designed to repair some of the damage that had resulted from past environmental exploitation and neglect. It resulted in construction of roads, development of new recreational facilities, soil and water erosion control, tree-planting programs, and construction of many utilities. Relying on more than 2.5 million unemployed persons, the program resulted in the planting of more than 2 million acres of trees during the 1930s. About a half million miles of fire trails, breaks, and forest roads were also built and maintained by CCC crews. Other CCC programs included managing the nation's national parks and forests, developing recreational facilities, and constructing hiking trails, public roads, and lodges.

The Roosevelt administration was also responsible for establishing such ambitious programs as the Taylor Grazing Act of 1934, which in effect closed public domain lands to homesteading, established grazing districts, and formulated programs to prevent overgrazing and subsequent soil erosion.

In the years during and immediately after World War II, few Americans were interested in the subject of land conservation, which fell into a holding pattern. Then, in 1960, Congress redefined the functions of the national forests to encompass all of their uses in the context of modern man's needs. The legislation stated, "The establishment and maintenance of areas of wilderness are consistent with the purposes and provisions of this Act."

This Multiple Use Act reemphasized Gifford Pinchot's concept of the unity of orderly integrated resource management. It recognized that wilderness management is part of forestry and is a compatible and complementary function of all other proper uses of the land. By this action, Congress made it clear that wilderness would no longer be considered something to serve only a single purpose. Instead, it would provide a habitat for wildlife, as well as various opportunities for hunting, fishing, scientific research, exercise, and other outdoor recreational activities.

## RACHEL CARSON AND SILENT SPRING

It wasn't until the 1962 publication of Rachel Carson's book *Silent Spring* that America and the world were finally awakened to the damage that had been done to the land and our environment in the preceding years.

A 1940s view of Norris Dam,
a project of the Tennessee
Valley Authority (TVA). The
TVA became a model for the
concept of government-sponsored
management of all the resources
of a particular region.

As a result of *Silent Spring*, increasing attention was focused on various matters of ecological concern. More than ever, the effects of large-scale land developments were being viewed in terms of their overall effect on the environment. The result was more governmental action on antipollution measures ranging from local funding to vast federal projects than ever before in resource management history. Congress enacted such legislation during this "Environmental Decade" as the Land and Water Conservation Fund, the Wilderness Act, the Water Resources Research Act, the Open Space Program, and the Clean Air Act, all based on legislation designed to protect our environment from the sprawl of urbanization and the pollution that accompanies it. Society was finally beginning to realize that man's actions in society are not without repercussions. Suddenly, increasing emphasis was being placed on the study and review of new uses of our lands *before* those uses took place.

Why such a sudden change in environmental awareness? Part of the reason may lie in the rapidly expanding world population rate and the dramatic rise of technology in world society.

## POPULATION GROWTH

By 1600 A.D., the world's population had reached 1 billion. Only three hundred years later, it had doubled to 2 billion. A scant fifty years later, it had reached 3 billion, and thirty years after that— around 1980—it topped 4 billion.

The rate of population growth in the twentieth century has resulted in the settlement of nearly all habitable parts of the world. The billions of people living on earth, more than 1 billion of whom are concentrated in various urban settlements, require a tremendous amount of energy to sustain the quality of life they have come to expect.

Today, it's estimated that the average U.S. citizen carries with him eleven tons of steel in the form of cars and household equipment while producing nearly one ton of waste of all sorts every year. Americans have become the greatest users of natural resources of any society on earth—those resources that the earth contains in limited and often non-replenishable quantities. Although Americans are less than 6 percent of the world's population, we use nearly 40 percent of its natural resources. And the imbalance is growing.

Within the next ten years, the world population will likely top 7 billion people. Urban inhabitants will total more than half that number, or 3.5 billion, outstripping rural inhabitants for the first time in history. Energy use will be thirty times greater than it was in 1900, quadrupling since 1970.

Nearly fifty years ago, the American architect and engineer Buckminster Fuller estimated that the amount of muscular energy required to produce the available supplies of power consumed by the average American was equal to 153 slaves working night and day. Today, that figure would probably be closer to 500 slaves doing what slaves have done since the beginning of time: struggling with domestic chores; cooking food; carrying people around; rushing in with fans and heaters; delivering the clothes, accessories, and jewelry they originally created; playing music; and removing garbage from the immediate vicinity. The only difference is that our modern-day slaves are no longer men but machines.

The spaces these machines take up, the power they use, and the wastes they give off are among the world's greatest polluters, continually robbing the land of the resources it requires in order to function properly: resources that are no longer available for use by anyone—or anything—on earth.

# CHAPTER 3
# BUILDING ON
# THE LAND

Asked what he thought about the subject of land, the late American humorist Will Rogers said simply, "They're not making it anymore."

Although Rogers was right, he stopped a little short of the mark. Not only are they not making it anymore, but there was precious little of it to begin with.

In proportion to the size of the earth, the layer of land and water covering its surface is thinner than the skin on an apple. Together with the air above it, this crust makes up our *biosphere*, that part of the world that supports life. It's a closed system in which all things are recycled and reused in support of the life process.

## LAND AS SOURCE OF
## WEALTH AND PRESTIGE

Throughout history, America and other Western nations have viewed land as a symbol of wealth. "A man's home is his castle" is a familiar saying that echoes the sentiments of many Westerners. The right to own land has been a fundamental issue since the very founding of America when European settlers immigrated from Europe in order to find the freedoms they had lost overseas, including the freedom to buy and own land. Once they acquired it, they valued their land highly and worked hard at improving it.

To these new settlers, land was both a symbol of freedom and a measure of wealth. It offered its new owners a reliable source of food and fresh water. It provided them with many of the raw materials needed to build shelters from the elements and to make clothes. It guaranteed them the kind of life they could not enjoy in Europe, where despotic rulers and members of the nobility were regarded as the only rightful landowners.

Over the years, landowners in America came to equate their property with power and wealth. If a landowner fell on hard times or illness, he could always sell some of his land to a neighbor for enough cash to see him through his troubles. In fact, as the number of people scrambling to own land increased, land became an extremely valuable commodity in the world marketplace. Although there may not always be enough land to be bought, there will always be someone eager to buy it.

Today, land is still regarded as a source of wealth, as well as a commodity to be bought and sold. "Buy low, sell high" is a familiar phrase that has made millionaires out of more than one land speculator, both in the United States and throughout the world. Land sale record books are filled with stories of speculators purchasing old, run-down farms for a few dollars an acre and selling them just a few years later for hundreds of thousands of dollars or more for residential and industrial development.

## LAND IN
## CONTEMPORARY AMERICA

Most recently, America has undergone massive land sales booms. Former scenic countrysides alive with trees and wildflowers and the call of countless birds have been chopped into neat parcels of suburban housing subdivisions. Many local governments, charged with the task of controlling the use of local land, have found themselves overwhelmed by the mad scramble to possess it and have been helpless to control the developing steamroller of the recreational and developmental land sale companies.

As a result, areas that once attracted people by their unspoiled natural beauty have turned into the exact opposite of what these people sought in the first place. Our scenic countrysides are slowly, steadily being turned into housing developments, theme parks, industrial complexes, parking lots, paved streets, and interstate highways. Once developed, it's nearly impossible to return an area to its former natural state.

But land development can be more than a visual blight on the horizon; it can be a threat to our very existence. Unwise development can lead to reduced water supplies by building over groundwater recharge areas: those areas that allow rainwater to filter through the ground to replenish the water table from which man draws water to drink. It can reduce the amount and quality of land available for growing the crops necessary to feed a hungry world. It can lead to reduced mineral extraction by allowing development in areas where rich deposits of valuable minerals are found.

America also faces disastrous overdevelopment of its wetlands and lands providing critical natural habitat for its wildlife. We've lost many scenic, historic, and environmental fragile areas. Natural bird sanctuaries, Civil War battlegrounds, delicate coastal estuaries, American Indian burial grounds —all have succumbed to the roar of the bulldozer and the opportunity for someone to grow wealthy. We face a dirth of unreclaimed surface mining sites that lead to soil erosion. We struggle with the problems created by urban development and the dangerous air and water pollutants it causes. We live with greedy land speculators intent on making a fortune from land development, often at any expense.

Of the more than 2.25 billion acres of land in the continental United States, about 35 percent is reserved for national, state, and local parks and forests. The remaining 65 percent is held by individuals and corporations. The ways in which this land is used vary greatly from one section of the country to another. Whereas cropland dominates the midwestern corn belt and northern plains, pasture and rangeland make up most of the mountain states and the southern plains. Forest areas are most abundant in the northeastern, Appalachian, southeastern, and Mississippi Delta states, as well as on the Pacific coast north of San Francisco, and large urban concentrations are scattered throughout the country.

Agriculture currently accounts for the largest single use of America's land, with about one-fifth of the nation's land in crops and another one-fourth in grassland pasture and rangeland. One-third of the land is in forests. Marshes, swamps, deserts, and barren land account for about one-eighth of the area. Urban uses require about 2 percent of the land; roads, airports, and other transportation facilities utilize another 1 percent.

## CATEGORIES OF LAND USE

Our use of land falls into four basic categories:

1. Satisfying our current needs, regardless of whether or not such uses exhaust the land's resources at the expense of future generations. This is a commodity- or profit-oriented approach to using land. The rate at which its resources are used depends on consumer demand and the competitive use of other resources. The rate at which land is used for the production of oil, for example, relates directly to the development of alternative energy sources such as coal, solar power, and thermal and nuclear energy. The more alternative energy sources being utilized, the less the demand for oil land.

2. Conserving land by using it in a way that maintains or renews its resources. This is called *conservation*, which means carefully managing use of our lands. Tree farming, for example, provides a landowner with income from the land while ensuring wood products for future generations.

3. Preserving land by leaving it in its natural state so that future generations may have the option of deciding whether to exploit, conserve, or preserve

the land, depending on both the value of the land to them and the needs of those generations.

4. A combination of all three of the above, perhaps the best and most realistic use of land: the sale of some land for houses and commercial exploitation, the use of some land for renewable agricultural purposes, and the preservation of some land as parks, forests, and designated wildlife areas.


If you were to visit many of the other countries of the world, you might be shocked to find the differences between those countries and the United States. In many places, poverty, hunger, and filth are overwhelming. Thousands of people sleep on the streets without any kind of shelter. Millions eat a bowl of rice whenever they can beg or steal enough money to buy it. They drink the same stagnant, disease-infested water in which they also bathe, urinate, and defecate. Their clothing consists of the discarded rags of someone more fortunate—or nothing at all. Sickness and suffering are everywhere, and the death rate is extremely high, especially among children.

There are many reasons for these people's tragic existence. Two of the most common are overpopulation and depletion of natural resources, which nearly always begins with the land.

Land is wealth. It's food production and shelter, a source of clean water and warm clothes. Once the forests have been cut and most other plant life destroyed, even the richest of topsoils blows or washes away, resulting in deep gullies cut by storms. The remaining cropland is extremely poor, barely able to support any growth at all. Those seeds that sprout are weakened from a lack of nutrients, and the plants quickly succumb to insects and disease.

In the United States, people still enjoy rich farmlands that produce bumper crops of food and fibers in excess of our ability to use them. Forests still extend as far as the eye can see. Rich mineral deposits lie just below the land's surface. Streams and rivers teem with fish, despite our past wastefulness. But these are quickly becoming the exception rather than the rule.

## NEED FOR PLANNING

If you were a land developer planning on building a brand-new community from scratch and wanted to make the best possible use of the land, you would begin by listing all the needs of the people expected to populate your community. Then, through a process of careful compromise, you'd evaluate the natural resources available on your town site to determine the kinds of development that would suit each place best.

You'd identify those natural resources of particular aesthetic or environmental value that would require protection from development: parks and green belts, for example. You'd limit the number of people who would populate your town by establishing various land-use and governmental controls to regulate urban growth and development. Finally, you'd arrange for strong enforcement of these controls to prevent uninformed or unscrupulous individuals from weakening your development plan.

Unfortunately, very few towns in the United States have been built with such foresight. In fact, most have been put together piecemeal with few or no guidelines to follow. The resulting growth from a standpoint of effective land use has been chaotic. America today has a shortage of several types of land, such as agricultural land on which to grow certain crops, adequate open spaces for recreational needs, and timberland for providing wood for housing and manufactured goods.

Throughout history, ancient civilizations prospered while their rich topsoils lasted. Once the topsoils washed or blew away, the civilizations crumbled and disappeared. The land was no longer able to feed the people, who ultimately fell prey to malnutrition, disease, and poverty. The ancient cultures of Athens and Rome, once the mightiest empires in the world, collapsed under the weight of their own land abuse. In time, the same thing could happen to another civilization, the richest empire in the history of the world—America.

How long will it be before these shortages result in a disastrous loss of invaluable minerals, fresh water, clothing, housing, and food? When will the time come when our imprudent use of the land results in the poisoning of the very air we breathe?

Some environmentalists, those specialists who study the environment in which we live, feel that time is dangerously close at hand.

In the book *The House We Live In*, Blau and Rodenbeck say, "We have learned that we are not merely in danger of being blown up; we are also in danger of being poisoned by the food we eat, gassed or suffocated by the air we breathe, burned to death by the radiation created for the purpose of peace, or drowned in a sea of our own accumulated filth."

There are voices in the wind, speaking barely loud enough to hear. We are on the brink of ecological disaster, they say. Our abuse of the land is already plaguing us. If we don't act soon, America could become just another statistic in the history books of the future.

The only question remaining seems to be *when?*

# CHAPTER 4

# PROTECTING
# THE SOIL

Webster defines the productive crust of the earth as *soil*. Many people call it dirt, ground, or earth. Whatever it's called, it's critical to mankind's very survival on this planet.

Soil is the part of the earth's surface that acts as a natural covering, like a jacket, for the planet. Formed by various natural forces acting upon rocks, vegetation, and decaying plant and animal matter over a span of decades, centuries, and even longer, it's the single most complex and important ingredient in our ecosystem: the very basis of life on earth.

## SOIL COMPONENTS

Not all soils are alike. They vary greatly in composition from one site to the next. The most common soil on earth—the soil in which trees, flowers, and food crops grow—is a mineral-based mixture of sand, organic matter, clay, and silt (extremely fine soil that's carried from one spot to another by moving water). These different ingredients are called *fractions*. One of the most important of all these fractions is organic matter, the amount of vegetable and animal material deposited in the soil. Through various chemical processes, this organic matter decays, producing nitrogen as a natural by-product. Nitrogen is an extremely important element necessary for the continuation of life.

Silt and sand fractions occur in different proportions within different soil types and serve as the main source of minerals needed by plants. These minerals include phosphorus, potassium, calcium, magnesium, manganese, copper, iron, cobalt, zinc, sulfur, sodium, chlorides, iodides, and boron. They're bonded together in silt and sand much the way they are in native rocks. But because these minerals are contained in much finer particles, they're able to decompose and break down more easily than they are in rocks.

The clay fraction is composed of very fine soil and mineral particles. It's the sticky substance in soil. Chemists call this stickiness *colloidal*. The amount of clay in certain soils determines whether the soil is hard and difficult to work or soft and easy to cultivate. Clay helps to bind different fractions within the soil together. When the soil is plowed up, the clay binds with the silt, sand, and organic fractions, which are turned up near the surface, where they're acted upon by sun, wind, rain, and various chemicals.

Under limited-production techniques used in America for a century or longer, farmers used to till the stubble from harvested plants such as corn and wheat back into the earth, a practice that resulted in the natural replenishment of organic matter and the minerals needed by the crops grown in the soil. As increased demands were placed on the soil through the production of increasingly larger crops, farmers developed new agricultural practices. They stopped returning organic matter to the soil. Since this new cultivation technique no longer provided enough mineral nourishment for the crops the soils had to support, farmers were forced to use various chemical fertilizers to supplement the losses.

## ORGANIC MATTER

But productive soils need between 3 and 5 percent organic matter in order to provide an effective base for crop use. Organic matter is mainly responsible for the rich black or brown color of soil and accounts for the loose condition of healthy soils. Organic matter is also the major source of phosphorus and sulfur, two important soil nutrients. In addition, it's the sole source of nitrogen. Organic matter provides the main energy source for many soil microorganisms that feed on the matter and help break it down into valuable plant nutrients. It also aids in increasing the water-holding ability of soils.

Green plants provide most of the organic matter present in soils. As these plants die, a layer of debris consisting of leaf litter, plant tops, and roots builds up. Centipedes, millipedes, earthworms, springtails, mites, and many other soil-dwelling animals eat this debris and break it down into simpler organic compounds. These compounds come from the waste materials of the animals. Microorganisms such as bacteria and fungi also help decompose organic matter as they feed on the waste materials in the soil.

Eventually, most of the organic matter in the soil is changed into carbon dioxide and water, two compounds that are used by green plants to make organic matter. Some organic matter doesn't decompose easily but instead remains in the soil for long periods of time. This more resistant organic matter is called *humus*, which is generally black or brown in color.

Organic matter in soils can be lost by overcropping (growing too many crops for the amount of nutrients available in the soil), as well as by burning and leaching (washing out) due to rains and water runoff. It can be restored by applying animal manure or returning the stubble and roughage from crops to the land or by using green manures such as winter oats, a crop that can be planted in fall and plowed back into the soil before planting food crops the following spring. Since cropland is being used continuously, it's important that farmers periodically return organic matter—and thus the minerals and nutrients so necessary to healthy plant growth—to the soil.

In its natural state, the amount of organic matter in soil varies widely, ranging from less than 1 percent in some soils to more than 5 percent in others. In the desert, for example, soils commonly contain less than 1 percent organic matter, whereas some high-peat soils have an organic content close to 100 percent. Yet, farmers continue depleting America's agricultural soils with little thought of the consequences.

Where will tomorrow's rich farmlands come from in a system that discourages the return of organic matter to the soil? Throughout history, farmers have paid little attention to the problem, and the agricultural soils throughout America are growing progressively drier and poorer in organic matter than ever before.

## MINERALS

Minerals are another important ingredient in soil. They're produced by the weathering of rocks. Weathering takes place in three ways: physically, chemically, or biologically.

Physical weathering occurs as various natural actions help to split the rocks into smaller and smaller chunks. Wind, water, ice, and temperature changes (which result in expanding and contracting of the rocks) all result in physical weathering.

Pieces of rock carried by wind or water wear down the surfaces over which they travel and are then broken down themselves. Ice masses such as glaciers wear down the surfaces over which they travel, depositing smaller rock pieces along the surface of the soil. Water that has filled the pores and crevices in rocks freezes, expands, and causes the rocks to break down. Rocks that are heated and cooled repeatedly by natural means also split into smaller and smaller pieces until they finally break down into soil.

## ENTER WATER

Unlike physical weathering, chemical weathering is caused by chemical changes in the rock minerals. The newly formed substances are usually more soluble in water than the original minerals and thus are more readily available to plants. Water is also an important ingredient in the process of chemical weathering since it results in hydrolysis, hydration, and creation of simple solutions.

During *hydrolysis*, water enters into a complicated chemical reaction with the rock minerals. The result is the breakup of the minerals. Although hydrolysis may take place in water alone, it happens more quickly when the water is combined with acid. This acid is usually carbonic (produced from carbon dioxide dissolved in water) or organic (produced during the decomposition of organic matter).

*Hydration*, or the addition of water to minerals in the rocks, frequently accompanies hydrolysis. When a mineral such as hematite (oxide of iron) is hydrated, it expands and softens, allowing the rock minerals to decompose more readily. These minerals may then be used by plants.

Water also tends to dissolve certain minerals more easily than others, combining with them to make a simple solution. This solution may then be absorbed by plants.

Biological weathering occurs as the roots of plants expand in rock crevices during growth. The roots produce carbon dioxide, which combines with water to form carbonic acid. The acid aids the solution of certain minerals and speeds up the breakdown of the rock into soil.

But soils lacking organic matter also lack moisture, making them less likely to utilize the processes of hydrolysis and hydration to produce simple solutions rich in minerals. Once again, the soils—and the plants that grow on them—suffer.

Of all the elements in the world, more than twenty have been found to be helpful to the successful growth of plants. The elements required by most plants in macroquantities (large amounts) are carbon, nitrogen, calcium, hydrogen, phosphorus, magnesium, oxygen, potassium, and sulfur. The elements required by most plants in microquantities (small amounts) include iron, copper, chlorine, vanadium, manganese, zinc, cobalt, boron, molybdenum, and sodium (see Table 1).

**TABLE 1**

**Nitrogen** stimulates above-ground growth and aids in the use of phosphorus, potash, and other nutrient elements within the soil. An excess of nitrogen can be harmful.

**Phosphorus** stimulates early root formation and plant growth while speeding up the maturity of crops. It also increases the ratio of grain and fruit to the stalk. Usually it's present only in small amounts and is quickly exhausted and must be replaced regularly.

**Potassium** promotes stamina and sturdy plant growth. Its availability is determined by the presence of other elements such as calcium, nitrogen, and phosphorus.

**Calcium** is an important nutrient forming a structural part of the walls of a plant's cells. It reduces toxic acidity and increases availability of nitrogen and other elements to plants.

**Magnesium** is usually found with calcium salts and has similar characteristics. It aids in the ability of plants to utilize phosphorus and is essential in the formation of chlorophyll, necessary for all green plant growth.

**Manganese** is also essential to normal plant development, working with magnesium to aid the formation of chlorophyll. It's required only in small amounts.

**Sulfur** is utilized by the plant in developing essential organic compounds, vitamins, and so on, and is usually found in superphosphates and other fertilizers that carry sulfates. It aids in the formation of chlorophyll.

**Iron** is required in small amounts. It's directly connected with the functioning of chlorophyll.

**Aluminum** is widely distributed throughout nature and is required by some plants and toxic to others.

Although a large number of nutrients are necessary to produce healthy plant growth, not all of them perform the same task.

As soils are continually used to grow crops, their nutrients are depleted and must be restored, by adding either chemically generated nutrients or organic materials to the soil. The only way a farmer can determine for sure which nutrients are lacking in his fields is to take a sample for soil analysis. The results of the analysis may show that the soil lacks 15 percent nitrogen, 4 percent phosphorous, and 8 percent potassium, for example. It's then up to the farmer to add these elements to the soil in the amounts required.

Besides nutrients, soil also contains small spaces or pores that may be filled by either water or air. The proportions of water and air in the soil are interrelated: as one increases, the other decreases.

All plants need water for growth. Soil retains some water after a rain. The water fills the soil pores as it moves downward as a result of gravity. Smaller soil pores can also be filled as water moves up through capillary action.

If you were to examine soil after a rainfall, you'd find its pores filled with water. If the rainfall continued, the excess water, called gravitational water, would begin moving deeper and deeper through the soil, eventually reaching the underground water table, a point in the earth at which water is constantly present.

After the gravitational water drains away, the water in many of the larger soil pores is replaced by air. As living plants draw water from the soil through their roots, the amount of water held in the spaces grows smaller and the plants find it increasingly difficult to get the water they need to sustain their lives. Finally, the supply becomes so low that the plants begin to wilt. Unless water is added to the soil, the plants will die.

## AERATION

Soil pores may also contain air. The air differs from that in our atmosphere in several ways. It's not continuously present, since it's separated by soil particles. It usually has a higher moisture content than atmospheric air. Its carbon dioxide content is also usually higher; its oxygen content is lower than that in atmospheric air.

The amount of air retained by soil depends on the amount of water in the soil. The air moves into soil pores not occupied by water. Since the soil water leaves the larger pores first, those pores tend to be the first to fill with air. As the soil continues to dry out, air enters increasingly smaller pores. Thus, soils made up mostly of small pores tend to be poorly aerated: that is, they contain more water than air. Clay soils are a good example. Since oxygen in the soil is necessary for healthy plant growth, clay soils are usually poor for agricultural purposes.

Imagine how frequent plowing and tilling of the soil destroy its ability to maintain pores of water and air. Yet, some farming practices require the soil to be tilled and plowed not once but several times during the course of a single season. How can soils so poorly treated be expected to continue producing bumper crops of food?

Mankind must begin taking better care of the soil, replenishing whatever nutrients, water, and air are removed by planting and plowing. Once a soil's air- and water-storage capacity is changed or its nutrients depleted, future crops are likely to be of poor quality and harvests will diminish.

But merely reducing the frequency of tilling and plowing and adding chemical fertilizers to the soil are not enough. It's also important that farmers use safe, nontoxic, nonpersistent fertilizers, since the elements in those fertilizers are likely to find their way into the groundwater table. From there, they may eventually wind up in our rivers, lakes, reservoirs, and even drinking glasses.

As valuable as water is to healthy soil, it can also be destructive. As farmers plow up their fields, they expose the surface to the elements. Such soil is extremely vulnerable to washing from rain, a process called *erosion*. As the rain runs off, it carries a certain amount of soil with it, leaving small cracks in the field's surface. These cracks eventually grow to the size of ditches or even gullies. As they get larger, they carry even more runoff and topsoil from the fields. Unless this process of runoff and erosion is checked by planting trees, mulching the surface, and returning crop residues to the soil, we may eventually pollute our most valuable lakes, streams, and rivers, and the soil that washes away will be lost to agricultural use forever.

# CHAPTER 5
# OUR CHANGING EARTH

In the early 1900s, newly developed technologies used in building tractors and other farm machinery enabled farmers to cultivate vast tracts of land more quickly and efficiently in the Great Plains states. The federal government encouraged them to do so, especially immediately after World War I, when food, natural commodities, and jobs were scarce.

During those years, rainfall was plentiful, crops were abundant, prices were high, and farmers prospered. Wheat farming spread westward into the semiarid (dry) rangelands, where more and more land lay ahead. It seemed as if there were no end to the amount of cultivatable land, no end to prosperity.

## THE "DUST BOWL"

But as farmers during the 1930s began plowing deep-rooted prairie grasses under the soil in order to replace them with shallow-rooted grain crops, they destroyed the land's main defense against erosion. Soon, the prairie winds drained the soil of its moisture, and the results were disastrous.

The winds began blowing slowly, subtly at first. Then, as the dry, hot days of spring moved into summer, they began blowing harder, relentlessly. Soil picked up in the Great Plains states was carried far to the east.

Geologists, called upon to analyze strange yellow particles that had settled onto the snow in a New England field, found them to be soil particles that had blown in from New Mexico, nearly two thousand miles away! In the following year, 1934, a gale-strength four-day wind storm carried an estimated 300 million *tons* of topsoil more than fifteen hundred miles from its origin. The skies were dark with soil particles from the wheat fields of Kansas to the metropolitan cities of New York and Baltimore. In Washington, D.C., great clouds of dust from the southern Great Plains settled on the president's desk!

That was only the beginning. Without fertile soil, farmers watched their crops fail. Entire agricultural communities went bankrupt. Food became scarce. Even when it was available, it was often too expensive for many people to buy. Farmers by the hundreds of thousands abandoned what was left of their farms in Oklahoma, Kansas, Nebraska, and North and South Dakota and set off in search of a better life. An estimated 100 million acres of prime agricultural land would eventually be lost—never to grow crops again!

That disastrous event was America's Dust Bowl, one of the largest contributors to the Great Depression, whose effects lasted into the early 1940s. It

*Men planting trees on a farm in Oklahoma in 1935. Their object was to reverse the damage done by the "dust bowl."*

was also a contributor to the establishment of the Soil Conservation Service, a division of the Department of Agriculture. Very nearly too late, mankind was learning that the land was not his to do with as he chose but rather to do with as was best.

Before long, the Soil Conservation Service was instructing farmers on techniques designed to reduce erosion while keeping their soils fertile. Such innovative farming techniques as contour plowing, terracing, and planting windbreaks help prevent soil erosion. Working the land straight up and down a slope makes regular furrows through which water can run on its way into gullies. By plowing along the natural contour of the land, the furrows act as dams to hold back the water long enough to allow it to be absorbed into the soil. Terracing the land by constructing ditches or embankments can also check the water so that it can be absorbed into the soil.

Wind erosion may be held to a minimum by mulching eroding ground with dead plants or by building shelterbelts, windbreaks to lessen the strength of and damage done by high winds. Farmers can plant rows of trees and shrubs at right angles to the prevailing winds to act as natural windbreaks to prevent erosion.

Eventually, farmers began following these new techniques—for a while. But as soon as food surpluses dwindled and grain was once again in high demand, many of them abandoned these procedures and began tilling all the land they owned or could rent in order to increase their harvests and boost profits.

As recently as the early 1970s, high prices and booming exports spurred farmers to expand and, in the process, take on costly debts. In an effort to pay

*Terracing is used in agriculture
to control runoff of water.*

off their loans, farmers put millions of acres of ill-suited land into crop production. In Montana, Colorado, and Nebraska, speculators converted vast expanses of rangeland into wheat fields and cornfields, depriving the land of the permanent vegetative groundcover that had held the soil in place for millions of years. The result: soil losses rivaling those of the Dust Bowl era, despite federal spending of close to $20 billion for erosion control measures.

Controlling erosion of fertile farmland is critical for several reasons. Many farmers discovered the most obvious one during the Dust Bowl: their valuable topsoils simply vanished in the wind. But there are others.

## COSTS OF EROSION AND WATER RUNOFF

Erosion strikes farmers where they can stand it least: in their pocketbooks. Assuming a minimum yield of cropland of 10 percent and fertilizer losses of $5 billion, the short-term, on-site costs of erosion total $18 billion annually in the United States alone. Altogether, soil erosion and water runoff cost the United States some $43.5 billion annually in both direct and indirect losses.

In addition, erosion deposits silt and soil in rivers, streams, and lakes, eventually causing them to dry up and die. As the water levels grow lower, first plants and then fish are affected. Soon, the water is nothing but a shallow breeding ground for mosquitoes and other insects.

But what causes the problem? Environmental engineers know now that the culprit is sediment, the eroded soil and silt that wash from fields and blow from the skies to settle in drainage and irrigation ditches, rivers, streams, and even large lakes. Giant water supply reservoirs in cities lose storage capacity. Since filtering the sediment out of the water is costly, water bills rise yearly.

Reservoirs providing water for hydroelectric plants clog up with sediment and eventually lose their capacity to produce electricity, and other sources of electrical generation must be found.

Nearly everyone has seen roadside graders scraping out ditches running along the roads. The graders are removing sediment that fills the ditches and plugs underground culverts, causing water levels to rise and roads to heave and buckle. Stream channels can clog so badly that they must be dredged with giant scoops or the bridges over them raised.

The amount of sediment dredged from America's streams, navigational channels, estuaries, and harbors each year is estimated to be a half billion cubic yards. The cost for removing this sediment is about forty cents per cubic yard, or $400 million a year, a cost borne by everyone in the form of tax money.

Sediment damage to all our transportation facilities, including roads, railroads, and navigational channels, amounts to many more millions of dollars yearly. When you add the cost of sediment damage done to houses, machinery, automobiles, streets, sewer lines, and wells, the total is staggering. And that's not the end to the damage.

Sediment greatly reduces the quality of our recreational facilities, affecting swimming, boating, fishing, and other water-based recreational activities. It destroys the natural spawning beds of game fish, kills their eggs, and reduces their food supply. In many small streams, sediment fills the deep pools that provide a refuge for fish during hot, dry seasons.

Commercial fisheries have also been affected. In the broad, shallow bays of western Lake Erie, fishing for yellow perch, cisco, and whitefish was once an important industry. Today, sediment from the fields of such nearby states as Ohio, Michigan, and Indiana has contributed greatly to the reduced number of catches of these fish. (In fact, cisco is on the endangered species list.) Similarly, sediment is causing oysters to disappear from Chesapeake Bay and other bodies of water.

Sediment is the direct result of erosion, most of which is produced by mankind's indiscriminate cutting of forests, overgrazing of grasslands, and misuse of farmland. The question is, how do we prevent it?

In addition to erosion, farmers in the northern Great Plains soon discovered a new problem. The shallow-rooted crops they planted (such as wheat, oats, and barley) failed to utilize all the moisture in the ground. The unused moisture picked up salts from rock formations beneath the soil. As the water moved up through the earth and evaporated, the salts were carried to the surface, where they accumulated. Once the soil became too salty, crops failed to grow.

Already, a quarter million acres of land in Montana have become too salty to bear crops because of saline (salt) seep. Many additional thousands of square miles are currently threatened in Wyoming and the Dakotas, as well as in the Canadian provinces of Alberta, Saskatchewan, and Manitoba.

Worse, still, there's no known way to remove the salts from the soil once they accumulate; that means these lands could remain infertile forever.

One way to prevent saline seep is to plant such deep-rooted plants as sunflowers and alfalfa, and more farmers are beginning to do that. Their efforts could save hundreds of thousands of acres per year from becoming barren wastelands.

Besides these problems, increased competition for land may well produce new problems for our agricultural lands. Strip mining, industrial and municipal use of irrigation water supplies, and urbanization—converting agricultural lands to houses, towns, and cities—are all taking their toll. America's love affair with the automobile has generated hundreds of thousands of miles of roads crisscrossing the land. Many of these roads show signs of severe shoulder erosion.

## POSSIBLE SOLUTIONS

In addition to such healthy agricultural techniques as contour farming and terracing—alternating varying levels of cropland—we need to enact laws requiring steep cultivated lands to be returned to woods or pasture. Raw, exposed stream banks can be riprapped—lined with large rocks—to prevent them from eroding. Willows and other water-tolerant trees and shrubs can be planted along the shores, and concrete jetties and similar retaining walls can be set where they'll do the most good.

In 1970, in an effort to enforce badly needed environmental laws, the Environmental Protection Agency (EPA) was established. The EPA quickly began conducting studies, making recommendations

to Congress, and enforcing new environmental protection laws. But although the EPA was an organization whose time had clearly come, its power wasn't sufficient to produce the desired results. Political infighting and selfish regional priorities prevented the EPA from acting on the great majority of problems it identified as needing immediate attention.

Today, America is experiencing a net loss of about 1.4 million acres of agricultural land a year. Our nation has only about 385 million tillable acres in all (excluding pastureland), 367 million of which is already being farmed.

As the world population continues to grow, how will we feed them? Once every available acre of tillable cropland has been planted and food demands continue to increase, what will we do?

One alternative is to create new strains of crops that produce higher crop yields per acre. Another is to reduce the number of crop acres lost each year through mismanagement and abuse. Another still is to find new ways to benefit cropland in the middle of urban sprawl. In Los Angeles, for example, the surrounding agricultural lands absorb city wastes. Wastewater is used to irrigate avocado fields. In other places, solid organic wastes are being recycled back to the soil.

*Field of alfalfa.*
*Alfalfa, a deep-rooted crop,*
*prevents saline seep by*
*absorbing water before it can*
*pick up salts from rock*
*formations beneath the soil.*

One promising means of encouraging farmers to use their land more wisely is to reward them to do so. The Conservation Reserve Program enables farmers to retire up to 45 million acres of erodible cropland. This aids farmers by reducing on-site erosion and off-site sedimentation, saving them money in both the short and the long run. It also guarantees them income for ten years on acreage entered into the program, actually paying farmers for land they set aside.

The program also reimburses farmers half the cost of planting permanent groundcover grasses or trees on eligible lands. These trees, which produce natural wildlife habitat and increase the aesthetic value of the land, become the farmer's property to leave in place or harvest at the end of the ten-year contract period.

A similar program aimed at preserving fragile wetlands, rather than placing them into crop production, has been initiated.

## LEGISLATIVE INITIATIVES

In 1985, Congress passed an important bill aimed at protecting our nation's farmlands. The bill requires farmers to protect their lands from soil erosion in exchange for receiving many government-sponsored farm benefits. The plan is based on a universal soil loss equation in which erosion from water is determined by the rainfall factor, soil erodibility, length and steepness of the slope, cropping and management practices, and conservation practices. Erosion from wind is determined by soil erodibility, ridge roughness, various climatic factors, unsheltered distances, and vegetative cover.

The plan calls for farmers to take five basic steps toward controlling erosion:

1. Farmers must identify those portions of their lands that are highly erodible. They can do this by checking their county's erodible soil maps available through the Soil Conservation Service.

2. Once a farmer has identified the highly erodible lands on his property, he must obtain a conservation plan. The plan is worked out with the help of the Soil Conservation Service and put into action by the farmer.

3. The farmer must actively pursue the conservation work outlined in his conservation plan by 1990 and have an approved conservation system in place on his highly erodible lands by 1995.

4. The farmer must refrain from converting wetlands into crop production.

5. The farmer must refrain from cultivating any highly erodible lands without first putting a Soil Conservation Service-approved plan into effect.

Although a number of farmers have objected to this plan because they feel the federal government is forcing them to change their farming practices, it's clear that voluntary programs don't work. By using U.S. Department of Agriculture funds as an incentive to ensure that farmers enact stricter soil erosion prevention measures, the entire nation stands to benefit.

# CHAPTER 6
# RURAL LAND USE

Bob Pharo flies a helicopter "gunship" for Helicopter Spray, Incorporated, of Lake Wales, Florida. On this morning, Pharo dips down to treetop level and squeezes the trigger on the yolk. Instead of bullets, his ship shoots hundreds of gallons of fine spray over the citrus groves below. The spray, dioxathion, is a pesticide designed to attack the red and rust mites that, in turn, attack Florida's valuable citrus groves.

Pharo is just one weapon in the war against pests in which farmers are engaged nationwide. From the citrus groves of Florida and the truck farms of Delaware to the rolling cornfields of Nebraska and the melon fields of California, farmers daily battle early freezes and late frosts, hailstorms and windstorms, excessive rain followed by drought, devastating insects, and disastrous blights. Add to that the farmers themselves, who often pollute as they plant.

Pesticides have been around for centuries.

*Airplane spraying fungicide onto
an orange grove in Florida*

Marco Polo very probably brought pyrethrum, a form of chrysanthemum from which a natural insecticide may be extracted, to Europe from the Far East. By 1763, the French were killing aphids that attack tomatoes and other crops with ground-up tobacco mixed with water. In the twentieth century, more powerful pesticides—both broad- and narrow-spectrum (killing either a broad range of insects or a specific insect)—emerged from chemical laboratories around the world.

The chemical pesticides farmers use today include insecticides to battle insects; herbicides to kill unwanted plants; fungicides to kill fungus; rodenticides to kill rats, mice, and other rodent pests; and miticides to kill mites. Most insecticides are either organophosphates or organochlorines. The organophosphates deteriorate rapidly once applied and thus are effective only for a short period. The organochlorines, on the other hand, persist in the environment, killing insects for long periods of time but also invading the environment and accumulating in the food chain.

## DDT

The most infamous of all organochlorines is dichlorodiphenyltrichloroethane (DDT), a wide-spectrum chemical pesticide developed during World War II that eventually grew up like Frankenstein's monster to turn on its creator.

DDT stopped a typhus epidemic in Naples, Italy, in 1943, saving thousands of lives, and brought such insect-spread human diseases as malaria, yellow fever, African sleeping sickness, typhus, and plague under control throughout much of the world.

But as the use of DDT spread, insects gradually developed an immunity to the chemical and increasingly larger doses were needed to destroy them. Eventually, DDT worked its way into the fatty tissues of birds and fish, which began dying off in large numbers. Eventually, the chemical was banned in the United States and throughout much of the world.

Herbicides, too, are in great demand throughout the world. Used to control the spread of unwanted weeds among crops, herbicides act on different plants at different stages in their growth. By selecting a chemical that kills weeds without affecting the crop plant, weeds may be controlled. But indiscriminate use of herbicides such as 2,4-D and diuron may also affect some insects, mammals, birds, and fish, and such herbicides must be prevented from entering the food chain because the damage they do may outweigh the good.

But pesticides aren't the only problem plaguing our urban lands. In the 1930s, beef farmers and ranchers used to free-graze a limited number of cattle on open rangeland. Steers reached slaughter size in thirty months. Their droppings became enrichment for the pasture or range.

Then ranchers realized they could raise more cattle more quickly in confined pens called *feedlots*. Today, feedlot steers mature in only fifteen months. But the waste matter generated by a lot of 20,000 head of cattle all clustered into a small space compares roughly to the sewage load produced by a city of 200,000 people. The problem of disposing of all that manure is a serious one that must soon be addressed.

Soil depletion is another problem facing farmers.

*Cattle being raised in giant feedlots*

The longer a single crop, such as corn, is grown on a plot of land, the more quickly that land will be depleted of certain minerals and other nutrients. Once it is depleted, future crops will be of increasingly lower quantity and quality until they fail to grow altogether. Applying expensive inorganic chemical fertilizers to farmland may eventually prove economically impossible for many farmers and could result in an unnatural buildup of certain chemicals in the soil to a toxic level, which may leach into and pollute the groundwater system.

## EFFECTS OF FERTILIZERS

In addition, high concentrations of fertilizers—both chemical and biological (animal manure)—eventually find their way into ponds, lakes, and slow-moving streams, where they produce large quantities of aquatic algae (phytoplankton). The algae eventually die, resulting in a loss of oxygen in the water due to the decaying process of the plants. This process, called *eutrophication*, has serious implications for other aquatic life that requires a high oxygen concentration in the water.

Eventually, the eutrophicated water fills with silt, soil, and other contaminants, leading the water to dry up and changing the ecosystem forever.

Loss of soil moisture is another serious problem affecting rural lands. This problem can be overcome—at least for a while—by irrigating the land, assuming water is available for irrigational purposes. In the United States alone, nearly 120 billion gallons of water a day is extracted from lakes, rivers, streams, and underground reservoirs for agricultural irrigation.

Irrigation, however, may cause serious problems in many localities, making it a questionable solution to the problem of feeding a hungry world. Irrigation may stimulate the growth of fungal diseases in newly moist environments, produce epidemics of parasites, increase salt levels to a point where soils may eventually become too toxic to support crop growth, and deplete underground water supplies.

Excessive use of underground water supplies for irrigation has exceeded the recharge rate, the length of time required for the water to be replaced, in some parts of the world. Depending on the location, a large population dependent on the water supply for municipal and industrial use may find insufficient water to maintain its quality of life.

In another instance, since freshwater deposits under low coastal areas often prevent salt water from leaching into and poisoning the freshwater table, depleting fresh water through irrigation may allow the aquifer to become permanently contaminated with salt water. In addition, in Florida, as well as in certain other areas of the world, removing large quantities of water from underground rock formations may allow the upper layers of the earth to collapse, creating huge exposed pits.

Still another problem facing farmers in rural America is one of economics. Faced with producing an ever-increasing amount of food for a growing world population, today's farmer has shifted from horse- and human-drawn farm implements to heavy mechanical farm equipment operating on fossil fuels such as natural gas, liquid propane, coal, gasoline, and oil.

Unfortunately, the massive consumption of these fuels both in the operation of the machinery

In a massive Mexican irrigation
project, a field worker siphons
water to growing cotton crops.

and in its manufacture has contributed greatly to the depletion of the world's fossil fuel supply. Mankind further uses fossil fuels to produce commercial fertilizers and to process the food once it has been harvested.

Recent studies show that the agricultural industry today uses more energy in the form of fuel to run its machinery than it produces in food harvested by that machinery. A by-product of fuel-powered machinery is increased air and water pollution.

These are all critical problems facing our rural lands. Yet there are solutions to these and other problems with which rural land managers must cope. In the case of nutrient-depleted soils, farm-grown biological fertilizers may be substituted for chemical fertilizers in many instances. In rice-farming situations, for example, the legume plant *Sesbania rostrata* was discovered by a French scientist working in Senegal, Africa, to transfer nitrogen to the soil in which it was grown, even under the flooded conditions preferred by rice. By rotating rice with this and other nitrogen-fixing crops, nitrogen levels on these croplands may be replenished safely and effectively on a regular basis.

## INNOVATIVE APPROACHES

At a fish-processing plant in Presque Isle, Maine, researchers have developed techniques for turning fish wastes into compost, animal feed, and biologically safe pesticides. Among the most promising of the new products is a nontoxic liquid spray manufactured by Biotherm International, Incorporated. The spray kills weeds, provides nutrients, reduces

Farmer plants oats in a field that had been planted with corn the previous year. Crop rotation helps restore nutrients to the soil.

The Colorado potato beetle, a
serious blight to potato crops

bacterial diseases, and wards off insects, including the destructive Colorado potato beetle.

Since early July 1989, a potato field on a hill overlooking Presque Isle has been sprayed weekly with a liquid called Biostar. Test plots of potato plants show that the Colorado potato beetle has hardly touched the treated plants, although unsprayed plots nearby have been eaten to the vines. The sprayed plants are greener and healthier than the untreated plants; this may be the key to the spray's effectiveness.

"It's a well-recognized principle in agriculture that insects are attracted to plants with yellowed leaves or that are weakened by stress," according to Spencer Apollonio, a marine biologist and consultant to Biotherm. "Our hypothesis is that the spray makes plants so healthy, bugs aren't attracted to them."

This is an especially important discovery to Aroostook County, Maine, which is the third largest potato-producing area in the nation behind Idaho and Washington state.

"We use twenty-eight different agricultural chemicals to grow potatoes in Aroostook County," according to William H. Forbes, executive director of the Maine Research and Productivity Center, "and some of them have ended up in our groundwater. If we can use a natural product as a substitute, the benefits to the environment are clearly apparent."

Maine's twenty-five fish processors once hauled tons of fish wastes to two rendering plants in the state and another in nearby Massachusetts. The wastes were converted into animal feed, eliminating a major source of solid waste. But as soybeans became the principal source of beef protein, the demand for fish products fell dramatically. The last of the rendering plants closed in 1988, forcing the fish processors to find a new way to dispose of the wastes.

Today, a plant in Boston turns those wastes into high-quality feed used in the raising of minks in the Midwest. Another plant in Bath, Maine, uses fish wastes to feed hogs and farm-raised salmon and trout. A third company in Portland, Maine, is developing a process to manufacture feed pellets for aquaculture and livestock from wastes.

The problems concerning the use of our rural lands, both in the United States and throughout the world, can be solved. But doing so will require the best efforts of research, industry, agriculture, and local and national government. Only by making solutions to these problems a priority for not only the large agribusiness companies but also the small family farm can we hope to save our rural lands, the lands that are literally the salvation of a hungry world growing in population with every passing second.

# CHAPTER 7
# OUR DWINDLING FORESTS

From earliest times of recorded history, the forests of central Europe were lush, dense growths of beech and oak so thick that in some areas sunlight never touched the ground. Some woods were so thick that permanent settlements couldn't be established until mankind learned how to clear trees by chopping them down or girdling them, removing a ring of bark from the trunk so that the tree would die. Once the trees were destroyed, fire was set to the remaining brush. After the fire died down, grain seed was planted in the nutrient-rich ashes—a practice that produced good crops—and livestock was pastured on whatever grasses and weeds grew along the edges of the planted fields.

Eventually, the forests grew back. When they once more became so thick that crops wouldn't grow, the farmers repeated the process or moved on, allowing nature to reclaim the land.

The practice of clearing forests in order to plant crops must have seemed a good one to early farmers, but it produced serious problems. Weeds, unable to grow in the shade of thick stands of trees, flourished in brightly lighted fields of grains such as oats and wheat. The weeds competed with the grain, robbing croplands of precious moisture and valuable soil nutrients and contaminating the harvests with their seeds.

Worse, still, clearing forests introduced a wide range of insect pests to the land. The Colorado potato beetle, for example, once thrived on forest vegetation. When the forests were removed, the beetle transferred its attention to man's crops.

Some pests even attacked man! As farming replaced hunting as the principal means of obtaining food, human populations grew larger and more stable, creating perfect conditions for the spread of parasites and such disease-carrying insects as mosquitoes, which could quickly reach epidemic proportions.

The practice of clearing forests in Europe reached its peak during the ascendancy of the Roman Empire. Once the empire fell, a period of civil and religious wars, plagues, and other tragedies occupied mankind's attention, and forests were once again allowed to advance.

European lands made their transition from forest to field and back again over a period of more than a thousand years, but the North American deciduous forests fell in a far shorter time. In 1620, American forests were so dense that a squirrel traveling from East Coast to West could do so without ever touching the ground. By the time the Pilgrims arrived in the New World, some Indian tribes had begun the practice of burning clearings in the forest and planting pumpkins, squash, and corn in the ashes. Soon the colonists were clearing their own fields, and by 1820, much of New England—once covered with trees—had become crop- or pasture-land.

It didn't take the colonists long to discover that New England farms often produced more stones than pumpkins, so settlers began moving west to New York State, Ohio, Indiana, and Illinois, abandoning their poor farmlands back east to the dense forests that cover much of New England today.

Cutting down trees, farming the land, and then abandoning poor or worn-out soil became a common pattern throughout North America, especially in the South.

## SCIENCE OF FOREST MANAGEMENT

The concept of actually managing the world's forests didn't take root until 1825, when forestry schools were established in Germany and France. Forest management didn't come to North America's apparently inexhaustible forests until much later, well after vast stands of New England and Great Lakes white pines had disappeared for good.

The major emphasis of forestry in Europe during the nineteenth century was forest protection from both overuse and fire. Then a young forester named Herman Haupt Chapman discovered that certain species of trees actually seemed to thrive after fires. Some tree species with "resistant bark" that protected them from fire damage actually grew better in the ash-rich soils produced by fires.

In 1909 Chapman concluded, "Fire always has and always will be an element in longleaf forests,

*A forest reserve in Colorado.
Forest management entails
controlled cutting of timber.*

and the problem is not how fire can be eliminated, but how it can be controlled so as, first, to secure reproduction, and, second, to prevent the accumulation of litter and reduce the danger of a really disastrous blaze." It was a sound analysis that would eventually change the way foresters throughout the world looked at fire and its beneficial effects on forest systems.

After studying the effects of fire on forests, foresters soon began studying *mineral cycling*. The roots of many hardwood forest plants absorb minerals easily from deep soils. The dogwood, for example, absorbs calcium, which it passes along to its flowers and leaves in the spring. When the leaves fall at the end of summer, the calcium returns to the ground, making it available to plants with shallower root systems. Dogwoods thus act as a pump, bringing calcium from deep in the soil to the surface, where it can be utilized by other plants.

In tropical forests, high daily temperatures result in quick decomposition of fallen leaves. Nearly as soon as a leaf falls, it begins to decompose, and its minerals are absorbed by plant roots and channeled into the growth of a new leaf.

When trees in a tropical forest are cut, the minerals are released faster than crop plants or the remaining trees are able to use them. These minerals leach out of the system, and soil fertility actually falls. Infertile soils make good breeding grounds for shallow-rooted weeds. As the weeds die in fall, the soil is exposed to the scorching action of the sun and a claylike substance known as laterite forms, eventually baking into a pavement-hard crust. Once formed, laterite is nearly impossible to break up, and areas that once supported lush forest growth quickly turn to worthless scrubland.

Several years ago, a large tract of rain forest in the Amazon Basin was cleared and cultivated. Within five years, the cultivated fields were virtually paved with laterite and useless as cropland.

In similar fashion, the prosperous ancient civilizations of Mexico and Cambodia probably fell into decay in part because of the destruction of their soils by laterite after clearance of their rain forests. The same thing could happen in certain areas of the United States.

## OTHER COSTS OF DEFORESTATION

Tropical deforestation also robs the world of many medical resources, oils, waxes, fibers, and other valuable commodities, as well as new sources for food. Currently, only three species of plants—rice, wheat, and corn—supply more than half of all human food requirements. Only about 150 kinds of food plants are extensively used, and only about 5,000 have ever been used. As we continue to eliminate entire species of tropical plants, driving some species into extinction, we're losing the potential to develop hundreds or even thousands of new food sources to feed a world population in which one out of every three deaths currently results from starvation.

Estimates made by the Food and Agriculture Organization of the United Nations in the late 1970s suggested that the number of tropical forests remaining throughout the world now totals about 2.3 million square miles, an area roughly three-

*Slash-and-burn techniques were used to create this rain forest banana plantation.*

quarters the size of the continental United States, or half their original range. Most of the loss of these forests has occurred during the last fifty years, approximately one-half to logging and the rest to cattle pastures, agriculture, and other uses.

Worse, still, pressures on the world's tropical forests are increasing yearly as a result of rapidly increasing population rates and spreading poverty. About 1.5 billion people, more than a quarter of the world's population, currently use firewood as a principal source of fuel. These people are cutting the forests down for their wood supply faster than the forests can regrow. Large areas of the tropics are experiencing a decline in forests due solely to the worldwide shortage of firewood and the degrading of soils caused by leaching and erosion resulting from clear-cutting.

Clearing our tropical forests may also pose long-term or even permanent problems for our environment. One of these problems concerns global climate.

Although most experts agree that the principal cause of increased carbon dioxide in the atmosphere is burning of fossil fuels such as wood and coal, a recent study conducted by several terrestrial ecologists concluded that nearly as much carbon dioxide is being released into our atmosphere by the destruction of the world's tropical forests. Increases in carbon dioxide result in increases in the world's atmospheric temperatures. These rising temperatures could eventually have a tragic consequence: the extinction of some species of plants and animals.

In addition, large-scale clear-cutting of tropical rain forests prevents some regional forest systems from recycling rainfall. That, too, results in rising global temperatures, more erosion, and loss of water supplies. Over a prolonged period of time, these changes in climatic patterns, known as the "greenhouse effect," may significantly alter agriculture and other uses of our natural resources and may even affect our health and very lives.

Why are tropical forests being cleared? Greed is one of the principal reasons. In Indonesia, vast areas of clear-cut forests are being converted to coconut or cocoa production or to agriculture. Clear-cutting there has swept over incredibly large areas, accompanied by vast forest fires that began burning in 1982 and are still burning today. In Borneo, more than 7 million hectares of forest has been destroyed.

In the high forests of Liberia, the Ivory Coast, and Cameroon, timber contractors go in to secure an export item for sale. They take out the virgin high forest, and immediately a flood of settlers follows the logging trails. The settlers plant cocoa and coffee and grow rice, so the farmers finish the job that the loggers began, turning fragile, unstable soil into wasteland.

In Peru, cocoa growers have chopped down large stretches of Amazon rain forest and are dumping millions of gallons of toxic chemicals and defoliants into the headwaters of the nation's streams and rivers. The coca growers, who produce nearly 75 percent of the cocaine consumed illegally in the United States, have invaded several national parks and forests, defoliated an area known as "the eyebrow of the jungle" because it's situated at the upper end of the Amazon, and destroyed an area estimated at over 500,000 acres of tropical forests, all in an effort to fill an increasing demand for cocaine in the United States and Europe. The coca leaf is now the largest crop under cultivation in the Peruvian Amazon.

The results of this agricultural venture are severe pollution, deforestation, and erosion of tropical lands. In addition, many species of fish, amphibians, aquatic reptiles, and crustaceans have already disappeared from the nation's rivers, lakes, and streams—all because an international drug problem has created a market that some people are willing to supply at *any* cost.

In addition, countless millions of board feet of tropical forests are cleared yearly to provide hardwoods for cold cash from industrialized nations. Yet, only one tree is being planted for every ten cut down, so these forests are not being renewed. Meanwhile, world consumption and production of forest products, especially newsprint and other paper products, are rising sharply. Experts estimate that the world may experience a shortage of these products by the year 2000.

## POSSIBLE SOLUTIONS

Virtually all of the food, timber, and fuel needs of the tropics could be met by using land more intelligently, leaving the remaining forests for biological preserves. Both the commercial logger and the fuel gatherer can grow the crops they need on lands that have already been cleared, and the cattle rancher could easily produce more than twice the current world demand for beef in pastures already available.

Plans must be made to preserve substantial natural areas to serve as parks and reserves and as a means for maintaining air and water quality and for erosion control. We must also strengthen efforts to create seed banks in which various species of trees and other plants can be preserved even if their habitats are destroyed. Along these lines, such multinational agencies as the UN Development Program, the UN Environmental Program, and the UN Population Fund can play an important role.

These are not inexpensive programs, and it's doubtful that developing nations have the economic resources to pursue such long-term goals on their own. That's why industrialized nations such as the United States, Japan, and the countries of Western Europe must help in the building, training, and employment of people within tropical countries.

The globe is no longer a vast, boundless area composed of special interest groups and individual nations. We have seen that what takes place halfway around the world can have disastrous effects on us. Only by working in conjunction with the people of other nations can we begin to assure the protection of our own culture and those of the future.

# CHAPTER 8
# OUR GROWING DESERTS

Desertification is the changing of productive lands into fallow wastelands. It's happening in Texas, where pasturelands have been invaded by mesquite, a worthless scrub plant that robs the soil of valuable nutrients and prevents grasses from growing. It's happening in Colorado, where pasturelands are succumbing to sagebrush for the same reason. It's happening in the African Sahel, where farmers continue to till marginal lands, and in the Sudan, Iraq, Egypt, and Yemen. The results are devastating.

The United Nations Environment Program estimates that 3.5 billion hectares (a hectare equals 2.471 acres) of land is currently at least moderately desertified, at a loss of about 25 percent of its potential productivity. Another 1.5 billion hectares is severely desertified, at a loss of more than 50 percent of potential productivity. The result affects nearly a billion people every single day of their lives.

Much of the world's desertified land was once lush green pastureland. Today it's barren sandy desert. A good example of the effects of desertification occurred in the coastal land west of Alexandria, Egypt, called the Maryut District.

More than two thousand years ago, the Greek author Strabo (66–24 B.C.) described the country west of Alexandria as studded with towns and cities. It was a healthy, thriving, growing community. Later the Alexandrian astronomer and geographer Claudius Ptolemaeus (Ptolemy) (90–168 A.D.) wrote of the great number of towns and villages in the Libyan and Maryut regions of Egypt.

Then, in 950 A.D., an anonymous Arab author wrote of the decline of Maryut in a manuscript: "Leaving Tarrana and following the road leading to Barca, one comes to Menas [Maryut], which consists of three abandoned towns situated in the midst of a sandy desert. . . ."

A French expedition into the Maryut province in 1798 described the region as a country of many ruined houses and walls, the remnants of once-large farms and orchards. A separate report in 1827 concluded, "The whole district is covered with ruins of towns, villages, cisterns, and wells dating mostly to Greek and Roman times."

What happened to Maryut? How did this once-prosperous community fall into ruin and decay? Some people suggest that great droughts might have turned the rich lands into fallow deserts. But writings from the last two thousand years suggest that Maryut had always been a drought-stricken area. Herodotus wrote around 440 B.C., "A grave portent occurred in Egypt; for there was a fall of rain at Thebes, a thing which had never happened before. . . ." Plutarch and other writers of the first cen-

*Practice plowing in Senegal,
in the Sahel zone of Africa.
A serious drought devastated the
region in the mid-1970s.*

tury refer to rainfall in the area as a remarkable event.

Various anthropological and geological digs in the area have since turned up a number of formed plaster walls applied directly to the gravel earth. These walls could not have been built in a climate with rainfall greater than the amount Maryut presently receives.

If there's been no measurable difference in the amount of rainfall in Maryut since Greco-Roman times, what caused the collapse of the area and its reversion to desertification?

Historians have recently discovered that the successful fig plantations on the sand dunes and olive plantations on the lower slopes of the limestone ridges surrounding Maryut were abandoned around the tenth century A.D. In their place, wandering nomads practiced uncontrolled grazing of their livestock. Even today, the livestock population in the area is three times greater than the capacity for the land to sustain natural pasture growth, and most of the animals are being fed through donations of feed and government subsidies brought in from the Delta.

Because of mankind's ignorance and indifference toward the land around him, an entire community reverted to wasteland. And Maryut is only one example of how mismanagement can lead to desertification.

## OTHER CAUSES

Yet, although overgrazing can result in desertification, it isn't the only cause. On the sandy plains of the eastern part of the African Sudan, gum arabic is an important crop. Growth of the gum-producing tree *Acacia senegal* forms part of a shifting cycle that begins during the cultivation period, when natural vegetation (grass and shrubs) is cleared, usually by burning. Grain crops such as sorghum are planted in the ashes during the rainy season, which extends for four to ten months. As the rainy season draws to a close, the fields are infested by the crop parasite *Striga hermonthica*, and the land is abandoned.

During this period of abandonment, grass and shrubs once again invade the fields. Within eight to ten years, gum arabic trees sprout and grow to maturity. During the next six to ten years, the trees are tapped for their sap. A second tapping results in the trees' dying off. As the dead trees fall to the ground, their trunks and limbs protect the soil from grazing, while tall, lush grass grows up among the branches. As the dry season approaches and the grass turns to tinder, the land is ready to be burned and the cycle begins all over again.

This delicate thirty-year rotational cycle has existed for centuries. But recently it has begun to break down. As local human populations have increased, their escalating food needs have lengthened the cultivation period. Grain crops are now planted longer into the dry season, preventing the gum arabic trees from reproducing as in the past. The grass, too, has disappeared, giving way to more drought-resistant plants such as worthless scrub and weeds. Much of the land has reverted to desert.

Overgrazing and overuse are two reasons for desertification, and there are others. One is too much rainfall—which may be surprising. Yet in a year of above-average rainfall, farmers may be tempted to extend their farming into areas that are normally reserved for light grazing. Pasturelands are pushed back, the amount of land available to livestock shrinks, and animal pressures on available pasturelands increase. As the farmers harvest their fields, the land is left barren, its surface broken by plowing. Dry-season winds blow away the topsoil, exposing the land to erosion. The result is desertification.

Another trigger for desertification is overirrigation. In past centuries, Egyptian sheikhs irrigated their soil by digging a series of ditches to the Tigris or Euphrates river. When silting and salinity eventually reduced the soil's ability to support grain and pastureland, the sheikhs moved their tribes to newer, more fertile areas, abandoning old lands to desertification while they began the process all over again.

In still other cases, irrigation water derived from shallow layers of fresh water that float above the main body of salt groundwater may become contaminated with salt. As the limited supply of fresh water is pumped from the ground, the salt water seeks to replace it. This contaminated water is drawn up and spread across the soil. As the water evaporates, salt deposits are left behind, eventually building up to levels that prevent plant growth. Millions of acres of land have been lost to salinization in Pakistan, Egypt, Greece, and South America. These once-fertile lands are today little more than great salt deserts.

Salinization, waterlogging, and alkalinization are worldwide problems. When land is exposed over long periods of time to water rich in salt and other minerals, the minerals eventually build up to toxic levels in the topsoil, preventing ground cover from growing. Without sufficient ground cover, the soil turns dry and erosion sets in. The results can be disastrous, both for the soil and for the people who rely on it to survive.

What happened in Maryut, the Sudan, and elsewhere throughout the Eastern world can also occur in the West. The Dust Bowl of the 1930s in the Great Plains region of the United States was triggered by a natural drought, but the disaster that followed was made possible by mankind's misuse of the soil. A sudden influx of settlers to the area beginning in the 1860s resulted in overplanting of grain crops and overgrazing of livestock on open rangeland. This abuse of the land eventually depleted the deep-rooted grasses and other ground cover necessary to prevent soil erosion, and the Dust Bowl resulted.

Although most desertification is the result of land mismanagement, that's not always the cause. In the early 1900s, a new catalyst for desertification was discovered. Since sulfur often accompanies ores of silver, copper, and zinc, smelting these ores to recover the metal has until recently resulted in pouring huge quantities of sulfur dioxide into the atmosphere, often with disastrous effects.

In Ducktown, Tennessee, a smelter located near a copper deposit released *forty tons of sulfur dioxide a day* into the air of this southern Appalachian valley. Not only were seven thousand acres of vegetation killed off and another seventeen thousand acres reduced to sparse grass, but most of the topsoil, exposed to rain without protection from ground cover, washed away, leaving a desert in the middle of one of the lushest forests in North America. Even though controls were eventually placed on the smelter to prevent the release of additional sulfur dioxide into the air, the desert remains.

## A GLOBAL PROBLEM

Desertification occurs everywhere. The United Nations Environmental Program recently estimated that as much as 6 million hectares of land are turning into desert each year. Areas of low rainfall, long dry seasons, recurrent droughts, and sparse natural vegetation are most susceptible. Land management programs, especially in arid and semiarid lands (those lands most prone to desertification), are needed to stop the process. But devising and enacting such programs is costly. Estimates of the amount of money spent on projects relating to desertification in the five years from 1978 to 1983 top $10 billion. Only one-tenth of that amount was spent in the field, the rest going for administrative costs.

In an effort to stop the encroaching desert, representatives of ninety-four countries met in Nairobi in 1977 and endorsed an ambitious program to combat the problem of desertification. Ten years later, the causes of the problem remained unaddressed. "The effects are misunderstood," according to Noel Brown, director of the North American Office of the United Nations Environment Program, "and the tools to bring it to an end lie around us unused."

Brown noted that the Nairobi conference estimated that investments of $4.5 billion a year were necessary to halt desertification by the year 2000. But only a tiny fraction of that amount has been made available. Annually less than $600 million is currently being spent in developing countries, according to Brown, and most of that is going toward such items as road construction and job training rather than soil management.

Equally disturbing, according to Brown, is that not a single country has put into operation a national plan to halt soil degradation. And of six regional projects recommended by the Nairobi conference, only two, a "green belt" project in North Africa and an aquifer project in Egypt and the Sudan, are being implemented.

That bleak picture was made even more depressing when Jeffrey Gritzner of the National Research Council described his personal observations of efforts in the Sahel region of West Africa. "There has been a relatively steady deterioration of environmental systems in the region," he said, "and a steady deterioration of food production."

Obviously, turning back the tides of desertification is neither easy nor inexpensive. A much better solution is to prevent further desertification through conscientiously applied governmental programs restricting land use and providing careful land management practices. Until that time comes, we're likely to see an ever-increasing rate of desertification throughout the world—and with it, lower food production, more disease, higher infant mortality rates, and increased deaths by starvation.

Can the world afford to wait?

# CHAPTER 9
# ENDANGERED SPECIES

Mankind is only one species living on earth. Yet we continue to destroy the natural habitat around us, habitat that has provided a home for countless other species for thousands or even millions of years. The prairies of the Great Plains once consisted of many different species of grasses, herbs, and animals. Now grass, corn, and wheat plus perhaps a few hogs and cattle dominate the ecosystem. Marshes have been filled in to make housing tracts, shopping centers, and industrial parks. Streams have been altered, land has been strip-mined, highways have been constructed, and urban sprawl continues at a frightening rate. All this development removes land from the natural habitat that preceded it.

Each year, an additional 1 million acres of land in the United States alone is placed into development. Where do the species that once thrived on that land go? Deer and opossum and raccoon and fox may simply move to the nearest adjacent natural land. But turtles and fish and trees and flowers

–101

aren't so lucky. They ultimately perish in the process we call development.

Every living species on earth has genetically determined tolerance limits. Once pushed past these limits, the species die. As more and more natural habitat is destroyed, the species that lived there find fewer and fewer places to live. They become endangered. They move, one step at a time, closer to extinction.

One example is the ivory-billed woodpecker, the largest woodpecker in North America. It formerly lived in the lowlands and swamp forests scattered throughout the Southeast. Its food source consisted of wood-boring insects that invade large, dead trees. As the virgin forests were cut down and replaced by sprawling southern plantations, the ivory-bill's food sources diminished. So did the ivory-bill. The bird has not been spotted for many years and may well be extinct.

But habitat destruction isn't the only factor threatening the existence of various species. Pesticides, heavy metals, poisonous gases, oil spills, waste disposal, and other by-products of mankind's activities also take a heavy toll.

In 1971, the International Union for Conservation of Nature and Natural Resources listed 297 species of mammals and 359 species of birds as endangered. Today, that number is rising.

*The ivory-billed woodpecker, once found in the southeastern United States, is now thought to be extinct. The cutting down of forests destroyed its habitat.*

# GENETIC DIVERSITY

There are many practical reasons why we need to guard against the destruction of the earth's plant and animal species. Each species represents a unique combination of genetic characteristics, called a *gene pool*, that enables it to adapt to certain environmental conditions. Sixty years ago, nobody would have cared if a soil-dwelling fungus called *Penicillium* became extinct as a result of the destruction of its habitat. Yet, quite by accident, Dr. Alexander Fleming discovered that the fungus produces an antibiotic that kills certain microorganisms. By introducing this natural bacteria-killing chemical into the human body, penicillin has saved hundreds of thousands of people from sickness and death.

Drugs such as streptomycin, terramycin, and tetracycline have been found in bacteria and in fungi. Some species of higher plants also produce valuable drugs such as morphine (from the poppy plant), cocaine (from the coca tree), and quinine (from the cinchona tree), which are required for the medical treatment of many diseases. These substances were first isolated and identified from organisms and then mass-produced synthetically. The science of pharmacognosy, a branch of pharmacy, is concerned with identifying chemicals in the environment that can be used to improve the health of humans and domesticated animals. Yet the types and numbers of chemical compounds still to be discovered remain a mystery.

Mankind's food production also relies heavily on a large gene pool. All of our crop plants and livestock have been domesticated from native plants and animals. The varieties of wheat and rice that currently play a major role in reducing starvation in underdeveloped countries are the result of breeding experiments using thousands of varieties of wheat and rice. If some of these varieties had been extinct, who knows what damage might have been done to the development of hardier, more prolific species?

The increasing amount of salinity in our irrigated soils may someday require the growing of new crops tolerant of higher levels of salt. If we decrease the gene pool available to biologists, we decrease the possibility of developing more tolerant crops. Once a species is gone, it's gone forever.

## ECOSYSTEMS

Although some systems are more important to man than others, each species on earth plays a role in the stability of our ecosystems. Not many years ago, the North American alligator was dangerously near extinction because of pressures from hunters and consumers who valued its leathery hide. The alligator's habit of digging depressions in the earth, called gator holes, results in a series of minilakes that are the last to dry up during a drought. These depressions serve as reservoirs and sanctuaries for aquatic life, as well as sources of food and water for birds and mammals until the drought passes. Without alligators, there would be no gator holes and wildlife would die off during dry periods.

Alligators also affect the ecosystem of the Florida Everglades by eating large numbers of predatory garfish. Keeping the gar population low makes such

game fish as bass and bream available to other predators, including human beings, who use them for food.

Although few species are so important to an ecosystem as the alligator, every species plays a role. As more species disappear, the system of checks and balances necessary in maintaining a healthy ecosystem decreases. The ecosystem is disrupted and is thus more subject to disturbance and potential demise.

Some people point out that extinction is a natural process that has existed since life began. Dinosaurs, after all, became extinct nearly 65 million years ago. But the point these people miss is that the natural process of extinction has been greatly accelerated by mankind. Although such species as the California condor and the whooping crane had been slowly dying out as a result of their inability to adapt to a slowly changing environment, the same can't be said of many species of wild cats, bears, and birds of prey. The short-term practice of continuing human exploitation will never outweigh the long-term practical value of preserving our ecosystem.

Once, the prairies of the Great Plains were among the most fertile on earth. During the last 150 years, mankind has greatly shrunk the scope of the prairie ecosystem while adding thousands of tons of chemical fertilizers and pesticides to the soil. When the land was too wet for agriculture, people drained the lowland soils to lower the water table for plant-

*The alligator plays an important role*
*in the ecosystems of southern swamplands.*

ing. What species have been threatened or lost through mankind's shortsightedness? Not only in the prairie lands of the Midwest but in the forests, lakes, reservoirs, and estuaries (coastal regions where salt and fresh water meet)? Before we can tell, we need more data that can be used to predict the effects of such intervention on the environment.

## THE IMPORTANCE OF WETLANDS

Our wetlands, marshes, and estuaries have traditionally been some of the first environmental areas to be altered. Mankind has long viewed such lands as breeding grounds for pesky mosquitoes and an inconvenience for farmers and developers. Yet, estuaries are highly productive ecosystems, serving as breeding grounds and nurseries for much of the aquatic life in the oceans. They're responsible for approximately 50 percent of the total food from the sea, food production that requires virtually no expenditure by humans. If grain farming were so inexpensive, no one would be starving today.

Wetlands are also important as nesting and feeding sites for waterfowl and other aquatic life. Without suitable habitat, these species would quickly become extinct.

During World War II, the artificial formulation of the pesticide DDT was viewed as a boon to mankind. It allowed farmers to increase their yields dramatically by killing those insects and other pests that compete with man for food. It eliminated malaria and a host of other insect-transmitted deadly diseases. It seemed a boon for life in developing countries.

Since the introduction of DDT to the world half a century ago, we've learned many things about it and about chemical pesticides in general. Not only lower animals and insects are susceptible to DDT's dangerous toxins: so is man. Human beings who have come into contact with the pesticide over prolonged periods have developed much greater rates of serious diseases than normal, including several types of cancer.

Yet, even though we had conclusive evidence that DDT was doing more harm than good to our health and environment, special-interest groups fought long and hard to postpone a general ban on its use in the United States. In the interim, several species of animals tottered on the brink of extinction, and many more have since gone onto the endangered species list.

Today, two decades later, several of those species are still fighting for their lives. We may not know for years to come whether they'll live—or perish from the face of the earth.

Of course, not all pesticides are bad. Some may be a necessary trade-off for the increased food production required to feed a hungry world. But indiscriminate use of highly toxic pesticides regardless of their effect on the environment can be deadly.

As an alternative to such broad-scale pesticides as DDT, mankind must develop chemicals that are toxic only to specific target insects. These chemicals must also be *biodegradable*, able to break down to harmless nontoxic by-products in a short period of time. Although these narrow-spectrum pesticides won't have the economic advantages of such broad-spectrum pesticides as DDT, they'll be environmentally safe.

Today science and technology are generating numerous alternatives to the use of pesticides in general. Experiments in genetic manipulation of certain insects preventing the insects from breeding and repopulating themselves are showing signs of promise. Other tests, like those conducted by Crop Genetics International, Incorporated (CGI), involve the genetic manipulation of the crop plants themselves.

CGI is currently following up a promising test conducted in 1988 using corn that carries within its vascular system a patented strain of bacteria. The bacteria have been genetically altered to kill the European corn borer, a caterpillar that causes about $400 million of damage to U.S. crops each year.

Other tests instill plants with new abilities to resist pests in the open field. Researchers testing these new pest-resistant plants claim that their work will lead to less dependence on chemical pesticides.

Still, conclusive results of such tests may be years—or even decades—away. In the meantime, farmers from Connecticut to California, from Bangladesh to Sri Lanka, continue relying on chemical pesticides to protect their crops from predators. Pesticide manufacturers continue producing their products—including DDT, which has not yet been banned in many countries of the world.

Once again, the question boils down to a simple one: What will determine our decision about pesticides: profit or environmental concern?

And while we're deciding, how many species will die?

# CHAPTER 10
## MANAGING
## URBAN SPRAWL

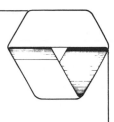

You needn't travel very far outside the city of Madison, Wisconsin, to find some of the richest cropland in America. Holstein and Guernsey cows populate thousands of the most productive dairy farms in the world. More than three-quarters of rural Dane County's land is devoted to agriculture. But that proportion is falling.

In 1987, the amount of farmland in rural Dane County declined by 5,000 acres to a total of 612,000. In 1988, nearly 1,500 acres were rezoned out of agricultural use. The number of farms and farmers has likewise declined. Where once corn, soybeans, and oats grew tall and green, today new housing subdivisions and business parks, shopping centers, and parking lots rule the land.

Dane County is being developed despite the county's policy of protecting its farmland. "Some of the best land for farming is also some of the best land for development," says Tom Smiley of the Dane

County Regional Planning Commission, "so there's a kind of trade-off."

Under the county's ambitious farmland preservation plan, some rural areas have been designated for development and the rest have been set aside for agriculture. Yet more high-quality farmland has been lost through the outward sprawl of the city than through any other factor.

"Probably more good productive farmland has been taken out of production by Madison and its policies of annexation than by all of the rest of the county put together," according to County Supervisor Lyman Anderson of the nearby town of Oregon, Wisconsin. As an example, Anderson points to the recent Madison annexation of eight hundred plus acres of prime agricultural land for American Family Insurance, which plans to build its new headquarters on the site just east of the city.

A few years ago, the land west of Madison consisted of fertile farm fields. Today, it's been overrun by motels, a bank, and several other businesses. Why is Madison so determined to gobble up much of the area's top farmland? Mostly, it's a matter of dollars and cents.

Although Dane County may be the richest agricultural county in the state, its farmers are nonetheless plagued by the same economic problems facing farmers nationwide. During the last decade, commodity prices have declined and the value of the average farm has fallen. The drought of 1988 magnified the situation. Real estate developers, on the other hand, are quick to point out that industrial parks and residential developments generate income, both from sales and from property taxes, income greatly needed by cities like Madison. The

*Aerial view of the planned community of Woodbridge, Virginia*

question is, How long can farmland continue to be phased out of existence before mankind faces a critical shortage of land on which to grow crops?

The problem isn't confined to Wisconsin. Not long ago, the residents of Washington, D.C., could escape the confines of the city and breathe clean country air in a matter of minutes. Today a trip to the country involves hours of driving on interstate highways or local roads lined with gas stations, stores, restaurants, shopping centers, hamburger stands, and houses. Subdivisions of clustered homes stretch almost to the Baltimore suburbs on one side and to Annapolis on the other. The forest that once bordered a local junior college is now a mass of shops called College Plaza. A few miles away, an entire town created by real estate developers rises from what used to be rolling fields of corn, grass, and alfalfa.

In Chicago during the 1920s, 2.7 million people lived on 200 square miles of metropolitan land. Today, that area includes more than 7 million people living on 3,719 square miles. While the population of Chicago has risen two and a half times during the last 65 years, the amount of land the city now consumes has increased eighteen times.

This is the world of urban sprawl, the spreading of urban areas until they overpower small towns and rural outposts. Since little vacant suburban land remains close to the city, the great American dream of owning inexpensive homes and businesses in the country is forcing people to travel farther and farther into rural America.

Although it's true that urban sprawl takes its toll on the amount of available farmland, it also generates other problems.

## RELATED PROBLEMS

Because rural homesites require people to drive farther distances to schools, shopping centers, restaurants, entertainment, and work, the amount of fossil fuels gobbled up in those trips increases. So does the amount of pollution the trips generate. One environmental report recently summed up the problem in this way: "Urban sprawl is the most expensive form of residential development in terms of economic costs, environmental costs, natural resource consumption, and . . . personal costs." The report pointed out that as housing density increases (as in urban dwelling), pollution from such sources as heating fuels and waste generation decreases. As housing density decreases (as in suburban and rural dwelling), pollution increases and the costs of providing basic services rise.

Managing water supplies alone poses giant headaches for many residential areas. Providing pure, clean water for drinking, bathing, and other purposes is costly—more costly per person in rural than in urban areas.

Existing sewer systems in rural subdivisions can't handle huge influxes of new residents. And the wastes from commercial and industrial developments make the problem worse. New sewers are expensive to install and environmentally risky to maintain. And rural sewage treatment facilities such as holding tanks, septic systems, and drain fields often break down, sending pollutants into the soil and sometimes right down to the groundwater table from which other rural residents draw their water.

Urban sprawl also affects the redisposition of

rainwater. As the number of suburban and rural residents increases, so, too, does the number of paved roads. These roads are highly impermeable to water. Large areas of pavement greatly decrease water's ability to percolate, or seep back into the ground, increasing the amount of runoff and downstream flooding. In effect, the water ends up where it's wanted least instead of where it's needed most. Airports, shopping malls, and even backyard patios all contribute to the problem.

Then, too, as more and more people stray farther from the inner city, the removal and treatment of solid waste—garbage—become increasingly difficult.

As far back as the beginning of mankind's existence, waste disposal was a problem. Even the mighty Roman Empire with its advanced system of freshwater aqueducts failed to cope with its own garbage, dead horses, and other solid waste products produced by more than a million inhabitants. Though the concept of the "city dump" had been developed five hundred years earlier by the Greeks, who forbade the disposal of wastes within a mile of their cities' walls, few societies adopted the concept.

Even as late as the fourteenth century, residents of Paris were allowed to throw garbage out their windows, a practice still in existence in some cultures.

The industrial revolution, which caused cities to grow rapidly, resulted in more goods being used and discarded, but there were no adequate waste-collection and -disposal systems. In the United States even in the 1860s, Washington, D.C., residents dumped garbage and slop into alleys and streets, pigs roamed freely, slaughterhouses threw nauseating fumes out into the air, and rats and cockroaches infested most buildings, including the White House!

In the early 1900s, several American cities began estimating and recording the amounts and types of trash collected. According to one estimate, each American produced 100 to 180 pounds of garbage (food wastes), 50 to 100 pounds of rubbish, and 300 to 1,200 pounds of wood or coal ashes annually. Europeans produced about half as much waste, making the United States the undisputed world leader in generating waste—a title we hold to this day.

After the turn of the century, New York City street cleaners were sent out in their sparkling white uniforms to clean the city of its trash. Juvenile Street Cleaning Leagues consisting of youths who volunteered to clean up their cities' wastes were founded in New York, Philadelphia, and Denver.

## THE THROWAWAY SOCIETY

By the beginning of the twentieth century, garbage collection efforts had improved, but disposal of refuse remained a problem. Cities with access to rivers or lakes often dumped their wastes there, but protests and lawsuits from beach resorts and neighboring communities soon stopped such practices. Some garbage was burned; other garbage was used as soil fertilizer or pig food. Still, most trash was dumped on vacant land or into marshes or other shallow wetlands. Though civilization had ad-

A landfill garbage dump adjacent
to Jamaica Bay in New York City.
Cities across the U.S. must confront the
worsening problem of what to do with
the mountains of trash they generate.

vanced considerably from the Stone Age, solid waste disposal had failed to keep pace. And the problem grew steadily worse.

By 1920, each U.S. citizen was throwing away an estimated average of 2.75 pounds of solid wastes a day. By 1985, that figure had risen to 8 pounds a day. And that's only household trash, not agricultural, mining, and industrial waste.

By the 1950s, the problem seemed to come under control as engineers developed a means of landfilling trash in which a day's waste was compacted and covered with a layer of soil. The result was called a sanitary landfill. Although anything but sanitary, the landfills nonetheless produced fewer foul smells and rats than earlier open landfills and dumps.

But recent studies have shown that our landfills are leaking toxic chemicals into our groundwater tables. Communities are running out of space in which to put the trash their residents discard. Mountains of trash rise higher into the air while the volume of solid waste continues to grow daily. So does the cost of collecting, hauling, and covering it. As if that weren't enough, most landfills today are operating near or even past capacity, and new, safe landfills are increasingly difficult to find. (Few people want a garbage dump next to their homes.) Suddenly, people who never before stopped to think about where their garbage was going are awakening to the problem at hand.

As urban sprawl advances, more landfills farther from the central city are being called for. Yet few are being created. Some rural residents have no legal access to landfills at all and must make private arrangements for the removal and disposal of their garbage. Often, it ends up at the bottom of open ravines deep in the woods, where hazardous material may leach into the soil and eventually work its way to creeks and streams and even into the groundwater table.

An especially effective means of treating solid waste is incineration, or burning. Even such persistent and toxic wastes as pesticides and polychlorinated biphenyls (PCBs) can be totally destroyed by burning at high temperatures. To prevent these wastes from escaping through plant chimneys to pollute the air, expensive equipment must be installed. This equipment isn't available to rural residents seeking to dispose of their garbage. Often, they simply burn their trash in cans or shallow pits, sending an unknown quantity of potentially dangerous pollutants skyward.

Increasingly, solid waste managers need to find ways to extend the life and efficiency of existing landfills or to develop new means to dispose of refuse. One way is to reduce the amount of wastes buried by first removing those materials that may have market value through recycling into new products. The most efficient way to do this is before the waste materials leave their source: the homes, businesses, and factories that produce the trash.

*A refuse combuster being installed near York, Pennsylvania. Heat generated by the burning waste can be used to create steam to produce electricity.*

Throughout the nation, many communities regularly separate their glass, metal, newsprint, and garbage into different containers.

During the month of December 1982, nearly 640 tons of newspapers, 150 tons of glass, 20 tons of aluminum cans, and 36 tons of steel were collected for recycling in the community of Marin County, California, just north of San Francisco. The program diverted about three hundred truckloads of garbage from the county's landfill monthly, reducing the total volume of trash by 6 percent.

Although the Marin County program is voluntary, a similar program in New Jersey, which produces 13.5 million tons of solid wastes a year, is mandatory.

In other communities, new types of waste-to-energy recycling projects are being built. In Dade County, Florida, refuse is taken from a holding pit and dropped onto giant conveyors that carry it to a 45-foot-long sorting device called a *trommel*. The trommel shakes the refuse, causing small objects to fall through holes onto another conveyor belt, where they're removed. Larger objects from the trommel are conveyed to blenders, called *hydrapulpers*.

Water is added to the trash, creating a mixture called *slurry*, and the entire solution is stirred rapidly. Centrifugal force carries heavy objects, including metals, to the container's walls, where they're removed. From the hydrapulpers, the slurry passes through further processing that removes small bits of noncombustible material and squeezes water from the remaining material. The resulting wastes are then conveyed to boilers, where they're burned to create electricity.

Ground-up garbage moves on conveyors at a garbage-recycling plant. The finished product, an organic compost fertilizer, is shown in the inset.

Recycling reduces the total amount of waste and reduces the need for new raw materials in manufacturing processes.

Among the items removed by the Dade County system are automobile motors, flammable containers (explosions happen regularly within the system but are controlled by venting), and cash. More than twenty-five thousand dollars in coins was recovered during the plant's first six months of operation.

Overall, the Dade County plant generates 30 percent of its income from the sale of by-products removed during the processing of the trash and another 70 percent from the sale of the electricity it generates. These revenues usually pay for the plant's operating costs.

Clearly, the solid wastes generated by urban sprawl can be handled more efficiently than in the past. And so, too, can such other problems of urban sprawl as loss of farmland, parks, and green belts, which can be protected through legislation. But the time to act is now, before it's too late. Once our most valuable farmland is gone, our mountains of solid waste are too large to control, and our groundwater tables have been polluted, it will be too late.

As the comic strip character Pogo once commented, "We have met the enemy, and he is us."

# CHAPTER 11

# LAND USE
# AND SOCIETY

Centuries ago, decisions concerning land use were simple. The local ruling monarch decreed what would and would not be, a decision more often than not based on personal benefit and the amount of money in the royal treasury. Sewage ditches for the kingdom? Yes. New wells for the peasants? No. Cobblestone streets outside the palace? Yes. New roads to the next monarchy? No. Free land for those willing to work it? No, no, no!

## BENEFIT VS. COST ANALYSIS

Today, our decision-making processes are far more complex. Unfortunately, they're not always more effective. Like the monarch of old, many modern governmental power wielders use cost as the single greatest determinant of land use. But instead of rifling the royal ledger books to justify the expenditure, today's computer-punching planners rely on a system called benefit/cost analysis to determine what will and won't get done.

Originally designed to weigh the benefits of two or more private-industry options in terms of benefits and costs, benefit/cost analysis has recently been adopted to justify public land use policies. Although it's an effective means of making such private-industry decisions as whether to expand the plant and hire more laborers or add another shift and increase existing work loads, it is inefficient and often outright dangerous when applied to long-term land-use policies.

When considering whether to allow a supermarket to be built on a large plot of vacant land or preserve the land for farming, local land-use planning boards often call for a benefit/cost analysis to aid in their decision. The results nearly always favor the supermarket, which generates the greatest tax base and most income for the community. In addition, the supermarket provides more jobs for local workers and fills a need in the community, providing a place for residents to buy food.

What benefit/cost analysis fails to take into consideration, however, are such concepts as land renewability, soil erosion, wildlife management, food production, and water quality.

Increasingly, intelligent land planners are beginning to rely less on benefit/cost analysis and more on environmental impact studies; less on immediate gains and more on the long-term advantages to the community and society in general. Although the supermarket may generate ten times the revenue of the farm during its first twenty years of operation, the long-term cost of removing the land from production—in terms of both dollars and effects on the environment—may be greater.

Even more frightening, how do countries with no land-use policies (most of the world's countries) cope with the shortsightedness and greed of local landowners and developers? The Massachusetts Audubon Society may have discovered one answer.

The society recently developed a program to help save the world's tropical rain forests, so crucial to the global environment. With help from several major corporations and foundations, American citizens may purchase an acre of land in the Central American country of Belize for just fifty dollars. The land isn't owned in the usual sense but is placed in a trust for the benefit of the people of Belize and the rest of the world.

Each acre of land purchased goes into a giant national preserve that will be managed by the Belize government with help from the Audubon Society there. The society hopes eventually to buy 110,000 acres to add to the 42,000 already purchased by Coca-Cola Foods.

"You can't walk into a third-world country and ask people simply to lock up their forests," according to the Massachusetts Audubon Society vice president, Jim Baird. "They're too poor for that. Conservation plans have to include the ability to make money," so current plans involve selective logging, limited tapping of chicle (the natural base for chewing gum), coca harvesting, and careful development of tourism, among other activities.

Could such a trust work in the United States? Most certainly. In fact, it already has. In 1985, the residents of Dutchess County in upstate New York formed a land trust similar to that in Belize: a private, nonprofit organization dedicated to preserving open space. The Dutchess County trust bought several farms and restricted their use with permanent conservation easements. Since 1985, the trust has resulted in the protection of some thirty-five hundred acres of county farmland and forests.

Public land trusts are quickly becoming one of the most efficient and promising tools for preserving land and preventing urban sprawl. The number of land trusts in the United States alone has grown from around fifty in 1950 to nearly eight hundred in 1990. But society is learning that trusts aren't the only way to say no to unwise land use.

By petitioning to add land-use measures to the ballot of local elections, an increasing number of Americans are flexing their political muscles. In California, a vote to close down a nuclear power plant is being placed on a referendum. If more voters say yes than no, the power plant will be closed and the land will revert to other uses. In Alabama, residents are voting on whether or not to allow the Texas city of Houston to dump its hazardous wastes on a thirteen-acre triangle of Alabama land. The results could send the waste to incineration sites in the face of growing opposition to land dumps.

Historically, America's public policy has favored private development of land in an effort to settle the frontier and establish a strong national economy. Today there are no new frontiers remaining to be developed. And demands on the country's limited land base are increasing.

As more roads, houses, and airports are built on the nation's most accessible and fertile soils, food production is being switched to less fruitful soils, resulting in increased food production costs eventually borne by the consumer.

As cities grow in size and their people are packed more closely together without sufficient open spaces, supplying them with clean water and air becomes difficult. As they move out into rural areas in an uncontrolled exodus, the cost of providing them with essential services skyrockets.

## GOVERNMENTAL MECHANISMS

Traditionally, decisions about land use have been determined by the highest financial return to the landowner. Many of the environmental problems the world faces today have resulted from these decisions. Although the public has exerted periodic influence on land use through public investments and taxation policies for years, there has never been a coordinated effort or single unified land use policy since the closing of public lands to homesteading more than a century ago. It's time, now, many experts feel, to initiate a new national land use policy to protect the public's interest.

The Tenth Amendment to the U.S. Constitution grants individual states the authority to manage both public and private lands within their territories. Over the years, the states have delegated much of this authority to city and county governments through various planning, zoning, and taxing powers.

The authority for determining local land use is usually given to a planning board or commission. This board is usually made up of citizens who serve without pay and are often appointed by the local head of government, such as the mayor. The board is responsible for representing all the people of the community in developing a plan of recommended procedures for land use, resource conservation, and development.

Citizens and property owners have the right to meet with the planning board or commission at any of its regular meetings, which are usually advertised in local newspapers. The board often obtains technical assistance from professional planners before reaching a decision. Public hearings are held before plans are made and ordinances affecting land use are adopted.

Individual states and even the federal government can also develop overall land use policies for environmental preservation and resource conservation.

## ZONING

Although a number of legislative tools exist for the regulation of land use, the most common is zoning. Zoning sets up areas or districts within a community in which certain uses are allowed. In theory, zoning laws protect the community by ensuring that certain developments—such as a new supermarket on land zoned for agricultural use only—don't take place. But all too often local zoning boards allow variances, or exceptions, to be made because of political pressure, the prospect of personal gain, or other motivations. To ensure that such special-interest considerations don't occur, individual citizens need to act as watchdogs in their own communities.

Land use issues are often the most sensitive for local governments, frequently pitting residents who want to preserve their land against developers who want to make the biggest profit from selling it. By pushing for careful growth management and intelligent use of space and natural resources, individual citizens can make a big difference in the way land is used locally.

But citizens can't act effectively unless they're well informed. Too often, members of a community are concerned only with those decision-making processes that affect them directly. To play a valuable role in determining the best possible use of our lands, we must become involved in decision making on a township, county, local, state, or national level. We need to attend land-use meetings, lobby for and vote on issues of importance to the community, volunteer to serve on local boards and commissions, run for elected office, and join such private groups as Greenpeace, the Nature Conservancy, the Audubon Society, the Sierra Club, and Environmental Decade whose goal of preserving the environment is well known.

If we have learned anything from the past, it's that the land we walk on, the air we breathe, and the water we drink are not inexhaustible. Yet, we often act as if they are. In the 1953 book *American Skyline*, Christopher Tunnard and Henry Hope Reed foresaw a problem they predicted would only grow worse before it grew better.

"Like the Mad Hatter at the tea party, who moved around the table using only the clean teacups and leaving the dirty ones behind, we Americans move on to new land once we have exploited the old. The central city has seemingly been worked for all that it is worth and then abandoned for the suburban fringe. What is perhaps more frightening is that the suburban fringe of 25 or 15 years ago is in turn being worn out."

America's land-use policies must not be determined by those special-interest groups out to make a profit at the expense of the environment. These policies should not be made for the benefit of local, state, or national governments and their representatives but rather for the good of the greatest number of people. The decisions we make regarding land use today will affect our lives tomorrow and the next day and the day after that.

# GLOSSARY

*Algae.* Primitive green plants, many of which are microscopic.

*Aquifer.* A layer of rock or soil that is permeable, allowing water to pass through.

*Biological control.* The use of a pest's own natural predators and parasites to control its population.

*Broad-spectrum pesticide.* A chemical that kills more than its target species.

*Chemical change.* The process by which the arrangement of atoms in molecules is changed to form different molecules.

*Compound.* A substance with fixed composition that contains more than one element.

*Concentration.* The amount of a component in a given weight or volume.

*Consumer.* An organism that uses other organisms as a food source.

*Contour plowing.* Furrows plowed parallel to land contours.

*Decomposition.* Breaking down of organic material into simpler materials.

*Ecosystem.* A unit of the environment that includes all the living organisms and physical features of the area.

*Energy.* The ability to perform work.

*Erosion.* The removal and transportation of weathered materials by wind, running water, or glaciation.

*Estuary.* Coastal ecosystems where fresh and salt water meet.

*Eutrophication.* A natural process whereby lakes gradually become overproductive.

*Fossil fuels.* The remains of once-living plants or animals that are burned to release energy. Examples are coal, oil, and natural gas.

*Fungus.* Primitive plants that function as consumers. Examples are mushrooms, rusts, and blights.

*Groundwater.* Water contained in subsurface rock and soil layers.

*Laterite.* A hardened, sun-baked tropical soil high in iron, aluminum, titanium, and manganese.

*Leaching.* The dissolving and transportation of soil materials by water seeping downward.

*Mineral.* A solid that is characterized by an orderly internal arrangement of atoms and a fixed chemical composition.

*Photosynthesis.* The process by which light energy is converted by green plants to chemical energy (food).

*Recycling.* The recovery and reuse of resources.

*Runoff.* Running water situated on land surfaces, such as rivers and streams.

*Salinization.* The accumulation of salts in soils and bodies of water.

*Saltwater intrusion.* The contamination of groundwater by salt water.

*Sanitary landfill.* A landfill consisting of layers of solid waste sealed between layers of earth.

*Strip mining.* A surface mining method that covers a wide area and is usually used for removing coal near the surface of the earth.

*Water table.* The surface forming the upper boundary of the groundwater reservoir.

*Weathering.* The chemical decomposition and physical disintegration of rock.

# BIBLIOGRAPHY

Aepel, Timothy. "Helping Farms Thrive—A Tough U.S. Row to Hoe." *Christian Science Monitor*, Aug. 14, 1989, 1.

Andrews, William A. *A Guide to the Study of Terrestrial Ecology*. Englewood Cliffs, N.J.: Prentice-Hall, 1974.

Barry, Patrick. "Cities Rush to Recycle." *Sierra*, Nov.–Dec. 1985, 32–35.

Belsie, Laurent. "Spotty Rains Define 1989 Drought." *Christian Science Monitor*, Aug. 18, 1989, 7.

————. "Water Quality Emerges as Key Issue." *Christian Science Monitor*, June 9, 1989, 8.

Bova, Ben. *The Seeds of Tomorrow*. New York: David McKay Co., 1977.

Carson, Rachel. *Silent Spring*. Boston: Houghton-Mifflin, 1987.

Cowen, Robert C. "Biotech Firms Test 'Designer Gene' Plants." *Christian Science Monitor*, May 22, 1989, 7.

Gebhardt, Maurice R., Tommy C. Daniel, Edward E. Schweizer, and Raymond R. Allmaras. "Conservation Tillage." *Science*, vol. 230, Nov. 8, 1985, 625–30.

Kiefer, Irene. *Poisoned Land*. Toronto: McClelland and Stewart, Ltd., 1981.

Lafchie, Michael F., "Kenya's Agricultural Success." *Current History*, May 1986, 221–31.

Mead, Margaret, and Ken Heyman. *World Enough*. Boston: Little, Brown and Co., 1976.

Pimentel, D., et al. "World Agriculture and Soil Erosion." *BioScience*, vol. 37, no. 4, April 1987, 277–83.

Pringle, Laurence. *Throwing Things Away: From Middens to Resource Recovery*. New York: Thomas Y. Crowell Junior Books, 1986.

Sinclair, Ward. "Keeping Soil Down on the Farm." *Sierra*, May–June 1987, 26–29.

White, Peter. "The Fascinating World of Trash." *National Geographic*, Apr. 1983, 424–57.

# INDEX